20.

The Industrial Revolution

The Industrial Revolution was responsible for the most sweeping social and economic changes in the history of mankind. Nothing like it has been seen before or since. Yet in one sense, it was hardly a revolution at all, for unlike the political revolts which took place in America (1776) and France (1789), no specific dates can be ascribed to it. The Industrial Revolution had no clearcut beginning or end, but was an acceleration of economic processes which had long been under way. In Britain, these processes started to gather momentum about the middle of the eighteenth century and made themselves widely felt during the next hundred years. Elsewhere progress was much slower. In the United States, for example, industrialization made little headway until after 1815.

The author begins by considering why Britain was the first country to experience an Industrial Revolution, and what were the reasons for its occurring when it did. He then looks at developments in Britain's textile industries; the impact of steam power; improvements in transportation; the new relationship between employer and workers; and the social effects of industrialization. Next, the spotlight is turned on the United States for an explanation of why mechanization and the factory system were so slow to be introduced there. Finally, we see Britain in 1850 established as "the workshop of the world." By this time, however, across the seas in Europe and America, other nations were already developing the means to topple her from this position of supremacy.

Other books for the Young Historian, uniform with this volume

THE YOUNG HISTORIAN BOOKS
Edited by Patrick Rooke

The Industrial Revolution

PATRICK ROOKE

MAPS BY COLIN JUDGE

RUPERT HART-DAVIS
London

Illustration sources

Science Museum, London:
19, 38, 55, 59, 61, 62, 83 and 98

Crown copyright, Science Museum, London:
24, 25, 40 and 51

Mansell Collection:
11, 17, 22, 26, 27, 33, 36, 42, 45, 47, 56–57, 58, 66, 75, 77, 78, 96, 100, 101, 103 and 104

Smithsonian Institution, Washington DC:
31, 32 and 86

Sheffield Public Libraries:
71

Rural Library 2

ISBN 0 298 79142 0

*Photoset and printed in Great Britain by
BAS Printers Limited, Wallop, Hampshire*

Contents

List of Illustrations

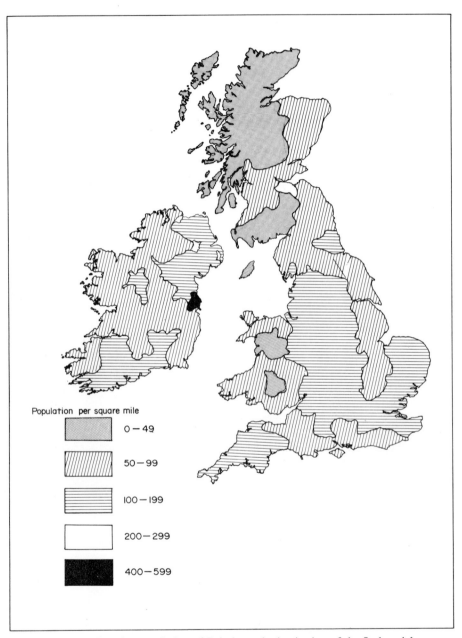

Population per square mile

0 — 49

50 — 99

100 — 199

200 — 299

400 — 599

Map showing the population of Britain at the beginning of the Industrial
Revolution, *c.* 1750.

CHAPTER ONE

How It Began

Although the Industrial Revolution is a familiar term to students of history, it is not an easy one to define. Difficulty arises over the use of the word "revolution." This implies a suddenness of change which is obvious in political upheavals such as the American and Russian revolutions, but is far from clear in the economic developments to be dealt with in this book. It is possible to locate exactly when the American colonies declared their independence of Britain, or when the Russians overthrew the rule of the Tsars, but we cannot say with any certainty just when the old industrial order was replaced by the new. Economic changes do not transform a country overnight. They have a gradual impact, influencing first one industry, then another; affecting this region before that one. It may be many decades before some new invention, manufacturing technique, or form of industrial organization has been adopted on a national scale. Because of this some historians question the validity of the term Industrial Revolution, though most would agree with T. S. Ashton that the phrase "has become so firmly embedded in common speech that it would be pedantic to offer a substitute."

There was a time when historians believed that they could give specific dates for both the start and finish of the Industrial Revolution. Arnold Toynbee (1852–83), for example, said that for England these were 1760 and 1800. Prior to 1760, he declared, little significant change had taken place, "the old industrial system" was still in operation, and "none of the great mechanical inventions had been introduced." Recent research has shown this view to be false. We now know that there was no sharp point of transition between medieval and modern industry. England was not suddenly transformed from a land where small cottage-based industries predominated into one in which manufacture was carried out by

No sudden break

9

machines housed in factories. Today the Industrial Revolution is seen as a long drawn-out series of uneven, often erratic, developments having no clearcut beginning or end.

All the changes that characterize it predate 1760, some having been present for at least two centuries before. There was no abrupt break in the mid-eighteenth century, but a quickening of processes long under way. This acceleration lasted for about a hundred years, though even by 1850 its effects had not worked themselves through the economy as a whole and sectors of industry still remained untouched by them.

Key changes   Three processes particularly mark the progress toward industrialization, each with its roots deep in the past. *First*, there was the introduction of new inventions and techniques. Contrary to Toynbee, much had already been accomplished even by 1700. Improved equipment was at work in a number of trades, including printing, shipbuilding, metal-refining, and ribbon weaving. Advances had been made in production methods affecting the manufacture of glass, munitions, and clocks. Even steam power, that mighty force which was harnessed to drive a variety of machines after Watt's invention of the rotary engine in 1781, was in use many years earlier.

Second, there was a growth in the size of productive units. This led to the development of the factory, an institution which was certainly known by the beginning of the sixteenth century. A poem tells of John Winchcombe, otherwise called Jack of Newbury, who had a factory where, within one room, "there stood two hundred looms full strong." But large-scale production was not confined to factories. Other kinds of industrial undertakings also expanded, increasing the number of workers which they employed. Coal mining was a good example. Between 1540 and 1640 the output of coal in England rocketed from a few hundred tons to many thousands of tons a year, a rise made possible by deepening and extending the workings. As a result, the labour force at a large mine now grew to several hundred. During the same period, a saltworks on the Wear River was recorded employing three hundred men while, farther south in Kent, there was a cannon foundry with two hundred workers.

Third, production became organized on a capitalist basis.
10   This was of two kinds. Under the one, sometimes known as

The famous Darby ironworks at Coalbrookdale, founded in 1709.

the putting-out, or domestic, system, the capitalist supplied
only the working capital, that is, the raw materials; the
labourer used his own tools, worked at home, and received
wages for his efforts. This system was well developed in the
English woollen trade by the fifteenth century. Under the
second kind of capitalist organization, the employer supplied
the fixed capital as well; the labourer attended the work place
of his master, where he operated machinery or used tools of
which he was no longer the owner. It was this form of organization which became increasingly characteristic of industry
after the mid-eighteenth century. But even here, the system
did not appear suddenly out of the blue. What may be called
modern industrial capitalism had its exponents well before.
We have noted John Winchcombe. Ambrose Crowley was
another example. Crowley, a seventeenth-century ironmaster,
carried on all the operations, from the production of bar iron
to the making of ironware, in his own works. At Winlaton, the
workmen, who manufactured goods ranging from anchors to
nails, were housed by this benevolent employer in a community
which had its own shops, chaplain, surgeon, and schoolmaster.

So far we have considered the Industrial Revolution as if it were concerned only with the British economy. Earlier historians often misled their students with such an impression. Certainly Britain was the first country to experience an acceleration in economic growth and, for a time, led the way as "the workshop of the world". But subsequently others, in both the American and European continents, followed Britain along the path of industrialization, each one in turn having its own revolution.

Having avoided one pitfall, that of viewing the Industrial Revolution in purely British terms, we must be wary of another. It would be equally wrong to think of it as no more than a phenomenon which affected a succession of isolated nations. Britain, France, the United States of America, and other "advanced" states were part of a world-wide network of economic relationships that also included colonies, plantations, and trading posts in areas where there were as yet few signs of industrial development. Changes in one country, therefore, had repercussions elsewhere.

Wars, often fought purely for economic gain, might disrupt relationships but, once ended, it was not long before former enemies were again trading with each other. This was so in the case of Britain and the United States following their war early in the nineteenth century.

The War of
1812
The war, which began in 1812, severed the close commercial ties existing between the two countries and had serious effects on both their economies. As a result of the blockade carried out by the British Navy, American exports slumped from $61,317,000 in 1811 to $6,927,000 in 1814, when the war came to an end; imports, during the same period, fell from $53,400,000 to $12,965,000. For Britain, though the war was but a side issue in her struggle with Napoleon, the interruption it brought to transatlantic trade caused dislocation to her industries and created unemployment. One speaker in the British Parliament commented:

It might be well to direct the notice of members to the proportion of trade these manufacturing places carried on with the United States, compared with the amount of their whole business. In Birmingham, it was supposed to be one-third or one-half; in Wolverhampton, one-half; in Sheffield, one-third; in the Potteries, one-fourth in value, and one-third in bulk; in Leeds, one-half or one-third; in Dewsbury, one-half; in Rochdale, two-fifths; in Bury, one-half; in Manchester, one-third or one-fourth; in Leicester, one-third; in Hinckley, two-thirds; and from the salt-works of Cheshire, 50,000 tons were annually exported. In all these places the demand stated had ceased; the consequence was, that those who formerly were engaged in the foreign trade, were thrown upon the home market.

It was not surprising, the effects of the war being what they were, that once it had ended there were many people in both countries who were anxious to reestablish trade links. This they did so successfully that by 1835 Richard Cobden could note:

England and America are bound together in peaceful fetters, by the strongest of all ligatures that can bind two nations to each other – viz. commercial interests.

There is no simple explanation of why it was in Britain that an Industrial Revolution first took place, nor of a second and related question, why this acceleration of change came just when it did and not before or after. Some have tried to find the cause in favourable climatic or geographical factors. Such theories do little to account for the timing of the Industrial Revolution, nor do they explain why other regions, similarly endowed, failed to develop as rapidly. Lancashire, which became the centre of the important British cotton industry, was far from being the only place in Europe with a moist climate. Though Britain had rich supplies of coal, so too did Silesia, where industrialization was delayed until much later.

Difficult questions

Another group of historians have found an explanation in the Protestant Reformation of the sixteenth century. R. H. Tawney has shown how England came to share with other Protestant countries a new code of ethics which, by no longer denouncing the borrowing of money at interest, was more in sympathy with the "capitalist spirit." J. U. Nef believes that the dissolution of the monasteries in England between 1536 and 1538 acted as a stimulus to change by opening up new opportunities for profitable investment. These theories, too, are less than satisfactory for they do not, by themselves, show either why it was necessary to wait two hundred years before an industrial breakthrough occurred, or why it was Britain, rather than some other Protestant country, that first experienced it.

Before an Industrial Revolution could take place anywhere, certain conditions had to exist there. Only by examination of these and the extent to which they were present in Britain during the middle years of the eighteenth century can we hope to find answers to the questions posed above.

Accumulation of capital The first prerequisite for industrialization was capital. Here Britain enjoyed a decided advantage over other countries for she had vast sums of money available for investment. Much of this wealth stemmed from overseas trade in which, with Spain and the Netherlands no longer serious rivals, her main challenger was France. Competition from the French, however, grew less as the eighteenth century wore on. The loss of Canada and India to the British weakened the French economy and was responsible, at least in part, for creating an adverse balance of trade, that is, an excess of imports over exports.

But capital alone was not enough to ensure industrial development. There had also to be men, driven by the urge to make profits, who were willing to invest that capital in manufacturing enterprises: men who had weighed the risks against the potential gains and decided, from a number of alternatives, that this was the best possible use to which they could put their money. In Britain, land had long been the most popular form of investment, for its ownership offered a steady, secure income, as well as carrying social prestige. But this changed after 1750 when an increasing amount of capital began to be invested in industrial undertakings. The position was very different in the United States, where, with a seemingly limitless supply of land, Americans continued to look to agriculture to give them the greatest returns on their money. Any capital left over was used to promote schemes for new roads and canals, thereby making it easier to market agricultural products. There was little to spare for the manufacturer.

During the latter half of the eighteenth century, Britain had both an abundance of capital and a class of men who were ready to use it for industrial purposes. She also possessed, through a well-developed banking system, the means of bringing the two together. This made possible the easy movement of capital. A person who had surplus money, but did not know with whom to invest it, could loan it to a banker who would
14 pay him interest. The banker was then able to relend the

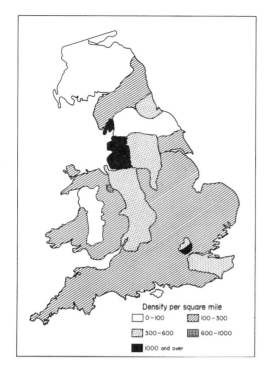

Map showing the population of Britain at the end of the Industrial Revolution, *c.* 1850.

Density per square mile
- ☐ 0–100
- ▨ 100–300
- ▦ 300–600
- ▦ 600–1000
- ■ 1000 and over

money, at a higher rate of interest, to any needy manufacturer who could offer adequate security. At the centre of this system stood the Bank of England, founded in 1694. (The Bank of Scotland came into being the following year.) By contrast, the French had to wait until 1776 before they had a comparable institution and even then it proved less effective than its counterpart in England, suffering as it did from excessive government borrowing.

By themselves, factors relating to capital are not sufficient to account for the Industrial Revolution. They do not explain why men were prepared to divert their financial resources into new channels of investment. What made these channels now seem so attractive? The answer can be summed up in two words – expanding markets. Unless there are likely to be more customers for their goods, businessmen will have no incentive to increase output or revolutionize production methods. For those in Britain during the eighteenth century prospects were promising. New demands for the country's manufactures were being felt both at home and from overseas.

Expanding markets

The expansion of the domestic market is closely bound up
with the question of population. Although the first Census of
Population was not taken until 1801, we have fairly reliable
estimates of the numbers of people living in England and
Wales during the previous century. These suggest an increase
of about a million between 1700 and 1750, and a more sub-
stantial rise of some three millions during the next fifty years.
In 1801, according to the census findings, the population
numbered 8,892,536, while by 1851 it was 17,927,609. Within
the last hundred years it had almost trebled. There had been
nothing like this rate of growth before.

The population of a country may increase for three reasons:
as a result of immigration, from a rise in the number of births,
or because fewer people die each year. During the eighteenth
century there was no marked rise in the number of immigrants
to Britain, nor did the birth rate change significantly. The
growth of population was due to a fall in the death rate, particularly among the very young. The decrease in infant mortal-
ity meant that more girls survived to an age when they could
bear children.

A population increase does not necessarily stimulate economic growth. We need only consider the situation in some
underdeveloped countries today to see that. However, in
Britain, there were other factors at work, some of which we
have already noted. Here, it did act as an incentive to manufacturers, especially to those who were concerned with the
production of clothing, food, and drink. Textiles, flour milling, and beer brewing became important pacesetters in the
process of industrialization.

Overseas trade Throughout the eighteenth century Britain's foreign trade
was mainly with her colonies and plantations. Its terms
favoured the mother country, from whom the colonists, barred
from manufacturing their own goods, were compelled to buy
all that they needed. Produce from the colonies could be sent
only to Britain and had to be carried in British ships. It was
largely in protest against these constraints that Americans
rebelled and declared their independence in 1776.

This colonial system enabled Britain to build up her overseas trade with striking effects. One has already been mentioned, that much of the capital used in the early stages of the
16 Industrial Revolution came from trading profits. It also led to

the development of a merchant fleet, second to none. Third, it provided valuable markets for British textiles and hardware.

Between 1750 and 1770 production for the home market rose by seven percent. Export industries, however, increased their output by eighty percent. The difference is not difficult to understand. Changes in home demand were associated with a relatively steady rise in population. Overseas demand, on the other hand, mainly expanded with the capture of completely new markets by war and colonization; it grew, therefore, by leaps and bounds. In the long run, it was the prospect of selling abroad which prompted the more revolutionary changes in Britain's industries. The manufacturer who could find new outlets for his goods overseas stood to make a fortune. At the same time, the risks were considerable, for the volume of foreign trade fluctuated wildly from year to year.

But manufacturers required more than markets for their goods; they also needed adequate supplies of raw materials. Once again British industry was in a favoured position, the textile trades being particularly well served. From her colonial trade Britain obtained valuable cotton, while at home she possessed an abundance of wool. The country's coal resources

A coalmine in Shropshire, 1758.

were plentiful and far in excess of those of her immediate rival, France. In addition, many British mines were located near the coast, making it possible to transport the coal by sea.

Transportation   The question of transportation was vital. Industrial development was certain to suffer unless raw materials were readily accessible to the centres of production and an easy means existed to dispatch manufactured goods to home markets or ports. This called for an efficient system of communications. In both Britain and France, during the eighteenth century, much was done to improve roads; in the former, the work was financed by privately owned turnpike companies, while in the latter, it was carried out by means of the corvée, a kind of forced labour. At the same time efforts were made to construct a network of inland waterways. Here the British were much in advance of their continental competitor. Rivers, like the Douglas in Lancashire, were deepened and made navigable. But it was the extensive construction of canals, carried out after 1760, which proved of particular value to industry. Heavy, bulky commodities, such as coal and iron ore, could now be conveyed more cheaply than by road. By the end of the century, foreign visitors were in agreement that Britain had the best transportation system in the world.

Workers for   At least half the population of Britain in the middle of the
industry   eighteenth century was in some way engaged in agriculture. But revolutionary changes were afoot in this area of economic activity too. The system of open fields, with land cultivated in strips, was being replaced by one of compact farms. This enclosure of land gave farmers more control over their own affairs; it became easier for them to carry out improvements, experiment with new methods, and generally work toward greater efficiency. But it had another effect, one that was of importance to the development of industry.

Enclosure was a costly procedure. Many small farmers could not afford the price of fencing their land or of replacing implements which had formerly been shared in common with other strip holders. They were forced to give up their farms. Some continued to work on the land as wage labourers. Others, however, decided to seek a new life in factory, workshop, or mine. They were joined by persons known as squatters, who had been displaced by the enclosure of common land. Without this reservoir of labour it is doubtful whether the Industrial

18

Revolution could have made such headway. In France, changes in landholding had a different effect; far from dislodging peasants, they tended to bind them more firmly to the soil. Although the total population was nearly three times that of Britain, French industry was handicapped by a shortage of labour.

Toynbee thought of the Industrial Revolution as the sudden outcropping of British inventive genius in 1760. But, as we have already seen, new machines and techniques were in evidence long before this. Nor were they confined to any one country. Scientists, in many parts of the world, had accumulated a considerable body of knowledge relevant to the problems of industry. There was a mounting and widespread interest in technical developments, fostered, during the eighteenth century, by numerous societies. These appeared in many European cities, including Paris and Hamburg, while in America there was the Society for Promoting and Propagat-

Encouragement of inventors

Newcomen's engine for "raising water with a power made by fire" was invented early in the eighteenth century. This engraving was made in 1717.

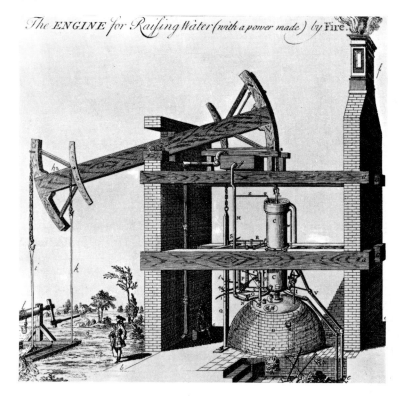

The ENGINE for Raising Water (with a power made) by Fire.

19

ing Useful Knowledge. Nevertheless, it was in Britain that inventors were in the most advantageous position. They benefited from being able to patent a new process or piece of equipment, a protection which those in many other countries lacked. At the same time there were a number of bodies established to encourage their work. Most notable of these was the Society for the Encouragement of Arts, Manufactures and Commerce, founded in London in 1754. As well as awarding money, medals, and other prizes, it publicized new developments and even opened a museum of machinery.

A sympathetic government   Finally, attention must be drawn to the positive role played by the British government in promoting economic progress. Throughout the seventeenth and much of the eighteenth centuries, during what is known as the period of mercantilism, the government operated policies which were designed to make the nation commercially supreme. The colonial system was established, navigation laws passed, and protection given to both agriculture and industries. The most important case of protection being granted to manufacturers was in the woollen trade; in 1700, for example, the government banned the use of finished silks and calicoes imported from India. In other countries, such as France, government policies were dictated by political, rather than economic, motives. Even when Britain went to war, as she did five times during the eighteenth century, her economic interests were always well to the fore. The memorandum of 1757, in which Lord Chatham proposed the conquest of Canada, makes this abundantly clear.

We have been considering the conditions which were necessary before an Industrial Revolution could take place. To summarize, they were: (1) an accumulation of capital; (2) men who saw industry as a potential source of profits; (3) a well-developed banking system; (4) markets for manufactured goods; (5) raw materials; (6) transportation facilities, making it possible to move both goods and raw materials easily and at low cost; (7) an industrial labour force; (8) inventions, and encouragement for those who made them; and (9) a government supportive to the needs of commerce and industry. By the mid-eighteenth century, Britain alone was able to satisfy all of these requirements. The scene was set for an economic advance, the like of which had never been witnessed before.

CHAPTER TWO

Cotton Reigns Supreme

The Industrial Revolution had its greatest impact on Britain's cloth trade. For hundreds of years this had been dominated by the manufacture of woollens, which provided employment for more people than any other single industry, with the exception of agriculture. Woollen cloth was the nation's leading export. During the second half of the eighteenth century, however, this began to change and a rival emerged to challenge its supremacy. This was cotton.

Britain's cotton industry had its origins in the seventeenth century. Located in Lancashire, and to a lesser extent in Derbyshire, it soon established close links with the slave trade which now became centred on the port of Liverpool instead of Bristol, as in earlier times. These links were threefold: traders often purchased West African slaves with cotton goods; slave labour was used on American plantations to produce raw cotton for export to England; and, in return, plantation owners bought Lancashire cloth for their slaves to wear. From its earliest days, therefore, the young industry was assured of overseas markets and a source of raw materials. At the same time, it began to prosper at home, where cotton goods steadily gained in popularity, for they were cheap and more easy to wash than woollen clothes.

The speed with which the industry developed is shown by the trade figures. In 1700 the annual weight of raw cotton imported was about one million pounds; by 1780 it had reached five millions and within five years had soared to eleven and a half millions. The export figures are even more illuminating, highlighting as they do the mounting competition between wool and cotton. *Imports/ exports*

At first, woollen manufacturers can have seen little cause for concern, for though the value of cotton exports increased ten times between 1750 and 1769, it remained insignificant by

A cotton warehouse, 1850.

comparison with the income from the sale of woollen goods abroad. In 1780 cotton exports were still worth less than £360,000. By 1785 they had risen to £5,000,000, but this was set against exports of woollen goods valued at £17,000,000. In fact, cotton did not gain the lead in overseas markets until the following century. This had been achieved by 1823, when the export figures for cotton and woollen goods were £23,000,000 and £18,000,000.

The domestic system   The making of cloth involves many stages, e.g. carding, spinning, weaving, dyeing. In the woollen industry these were mainly carried out in the home, with all the members of the family taking part. Wealthy clothiers often controlled the trade, touring the countryside with their strings of pack horses. They put out wool to the various households, returning later when the work had been completed. Although the production of woollen cloth was maintained at a high level throughout the eighteenth century, this "domestic system" was far from perfect. One weakness was the time that was wasted in shifting partly finished products from household to household. Another arose from the fact that, being always on the move, clothiers were unable to supervise the work while it was actually being undertaken.

22   Originally the cotton industry had been organized in a

similar way but, after 1750, and unlike wool, it began to move from a domestic to a factory system. But the transition was slower than historians once thought, progress being uneven in the different manufacturing processes. Weaving, for example, advanced less rapidly than spinning. The rate of development was closely bound up with the degree to which a particular process became mechanized. Before considering what new machinery was now brought into use, a note of caution is necessary. Much has been written about the outstanding success of certain inventions; without denying the importance of their long-term effects, it is well to remember that, when first introduced, these machines were often very crude and in need of many refinements before they could be made to operate efficiently.

Textile manufacturers, whether of woollens, cottons, or silks, were faced with a difficult problem. They had to ensure that the spinners produced enough yarn to keep the looms of the weavers fully occupied. The first of the important textile inventions, a flying shuttle, designed and patented by John Kay in 1733, far from easing this problem, made it more acute, for its effect was to speed up the weaving process. It was no longer necessary for a weaver to throw the shuttle from hand to hand; now he could send it automatically from one side of the loom to the other. Apart from being quicker, this meant that a single operator was able to weave cloth of greater width. Intended for the woollen industry, Kay's shuttle was, by the 1760's, in use on cotton looms as well.

Even before the arrival of the flying shuttle, four spinners had been required to keep one weaver supplied with yarn. Following Kay's invention the balance between the two processes was further upset. In consequence, inventors redoubled their efforts to perfect a machine that was capable of spinning more than a single thread. As early as 1738 John Wyatt and Lewis Paul produced a spinning machine that made fibre into threads by passing it through a series of rollers. Although employed in a mill at Northampton, where it was powered by water, the invention did not prove a practical success and many years were to pass before a satisfactory solution was found to the problem.

A breakthrough came in 1767 when James Hargreaves, a carpenter and loom maker, invented a wheel which was 23

Spinning jenny.
This model could
spin sixteen threads
at one time.

capable of spinning eight threads at one time. He called his machine a *jenny*, after his wife. But though later jennies were able to accommodate as many as a hundred spindles, the invention had a serious weakness. It could only spin yarn which was suitable for use as weft. For the warp something stronger was needed. It took two further inventions, Arkwright's water frame and Crompton's mule, to remedy this deficiency.

Richard
Arkwright
    The water frame, patented in 1769, was an intricate machine which, by making use of rollers rotating at different speeds, produced yarn that was both hard and tough. Although associated with the name of Richard Arkwright, it was probably the work of a certain Thomas Highs (or Hayes). Arkwright, a barber and wig maker by trade, gained notoriety for stealing the ideas of other men. He was forced to defend his patent rights in a series of lawsuits which culminated in 1785 with Parliament revoking them all. Despite this loss, Arkwright became the outstanding capitalist in the cotton industry, for

24

what he lacked in inventive ability, this unscrupulous operator more than made up for in business acumen. Unlike Hargreaves and many other "real inventors," Arkwright died a rich man. His spinning mill at Cromford, opened in 1771, was soon employing three hundred workers. It was but one of a number in which he acquired interests.

But though Arkwright owed much of his success to the use he made of the water frame, the machine was far from perfect, for the yarn that it manufactured was still coarse. It was left to Samuel Crompton to produce thread with a finer texture. This he achieved in 1779 by combining the principles of the jenny with those of the water frame. Because the resulting machine was a crossbred, it became known as a *mule*.

The effects of the various types of spinning machine were considerable. Supplies of yarn were greatly increased, while the actual cost of production was lowered. In consequence, the spinning mills were now in danger of manufacturing more thread than the weavers were able to handle. There was an

Power looms

25

Carding machines at work in a cotton factory during the 1830's.

urgent need to step up the output of cloth. This called for an invention which would revolutionize the weaving process. In 1785 Edmund Cartwright, a clergyman, designed a power loom which, though having many defects, did seem promising. First Cartwright, then others, brought out improved versions of the machine, but many years were to pass before a really satisfactory model appeared. By contrast with the spinning machines, therefore, the power loom made slow progress and even in 1813 there were probably no more than 2,400 in the country, as against nearly a hundred times that number of hand-operated looms.

Progress in carding, bleaching and printing

New developments were not restricted to spinning and weaving. Before any cotton could be spun it had to be combed to remove all lumps, a process known as carding. In 1748 Lewis Paul patented a cylindrical carding machine, some of which had worked alongside his roller-spinners at the mill in Northampton. Among the disputed patents taken out nearly thirty years later by Arkwright was one for a carding machine consisting of three cylinders of varying diameters, each covered with bent metal teeth. This machine, according to

26

Calico printing, 1835.

evidence brought against him at the trial of 1785, was almost identical to one invented by a Daniel Bourne at a much earlier date. But, whatever its origins, it soon proved of value by mechanizing what had previously been a tedious hand operation.

Improvements were also made in the finishing processes of bleaching, dyeing, and printing. It had long been customary to bleach cloth by soaking it in sour milk and then leaving it exposed to the elements. As early as the 1740's John Roebuck had tried to speed up the process by making use of sulphuric acid, but it was not until 1785 that a successful method was found. This was by the French chemist Berthollet, who employed chlorine as a bleaching agent. News of his discovery was brought to England by James Watt the following year. At the same time fabrics were being made brighter by the use of new colours and dyes. As for printing, this was transformed by Thomas Bell who, in 1783, invented a revolving press which soon replaced the method of hand-stamping cloth.

Why were the new machines introduced into the cotton rather than the woollen, industry? There were several reasons. 27

Why the cotton industry? First, wool was a softer fibre than cotton and less suitable for use on the early, crude machinery. Second, information about new techniques spread more easily among those who worked in cotton, for the industry was confined to one part of England; in contrast, the manufacture of woollen cloth took place in a large number of areas, to some of which the knowledge of technical improvements seeped through very slowly. Third, being relatively new itself, the cotton industry responded favourably to fresh ideas; unlike the woollen trade, its operations were not shackled with regulations and practices which had become hallowed by time. In a sense, the woollen industry was a victim of its own long and successful past. Finally, cotton benefited more than wool from the growing demand for textiles, both home and overseas buyers showing an increasing preference for the lighter fabrics of Lancashire.

The factory system It is often said that the Industrial Revolution was responsible for the factory system. Of course, to a large extent this is true. But like most generalizations, the statement does not tell the whole truth. It masks the fact, for example, that some factories were in operation before 1750. It also implies that by 1850 the factory system had spread more rapidly, and to more industries, than was actually the case.

Silk Factory production did not begin with the cotton industry. Even among textiles cotton was not the first to be organized in this way. Many years before there had been woollen manufactories like that of John Winchcombe. However, these were no more than isolated instances in a trade that was still predominantly domestic. Of greater significance were developments in the silk-throwing industry, where factories were already well established by the mid-eighteenth century.

The first silk mill was set up in 1719 by Thomas Lombe. Situated near Derby, it was a large building, five hundred feet long, five or six storeys high, with four hundred and sixty winddows. Inside were tall, cylindrical-shaped machines which made silk thread by twisting together the filament from the cocoons.

The story of those machines is fascinating. John Lombe, the brother of Thomas, having heard a rumour that a silk-throwing machine was in operation in Italy, decided to go and investigate. But when he arrived there, he discovered that the invention was a closely guarded secret and not for foreign eyes. Nevertheless, he was an enterprising young man and

28

somehow obtained a copy of its design which he managed to smuggle out of the country. This early example of industrial sabotage brought a fortune to Thomas – within fifteen years he had made £120,000 – but probably cost John his life. Many people believed that his death, a few years later, was the result of poisoning carried out at the instigation of those he had robbed.

Where the Lombes had led, others followed, and before very long a number of silk-throwing mills had come into existence, some employing as many as eight hundred workers. Why then, in spite of this promising start, did silk fail to expand in the same way as cotton? In brief, there was never more than a limited demand for silk, a luxury article. For half a century, improvements in the manufacture of silk thread had little effect on the methods used by those who carried out the weaving and finishing processes.

Despite the progress in silk-throwing by 1750, despite the rapid spread of cotton-spinning mills after 1780, it was not until the middle of the nineteenth century that all the textile trades were moving toward factory production. The introduction of the factory system, which came even later to many other industries, was more in the nature of an evolutionary, rather than a revolutionary, change. *An evolutionary change*

There are at least four reasons for the slow progress of factory production. First, not all the new machinery was dependent upon this kind of organization. Important inventions like Kay's shuttle and the first jennies of Hargreaves could easily be used in the home. It was not until the advent of large, power-driven machines that factories became essential. Second, when these machines did appear, they suffered from numerous teething troubles and broke down with alarming frequency. It was not surprising that manufacturers preferred a domestic system, which did at least work, to a mode of operations that seemed inefficient and unreliable. They waited until the machines had been improved and were more trustworthy. Third, to reorganize production on a factory basis was both a costly and hazardous business. Although it might promise high profits, the step also brought considerable risks for, if there was a slump, a manufacturer would find his capital tied up in buildings and expensive equipment which had substantially dropped in value.

Finally, during the early stages of the Industrial Revolution, there was a great deal of hostility among the workers toward both factories and new machinery, reflecting a deep-rooted suspicion of change. Dislike of the factory was related to working conditions. Though not necessarily harder than it had been in the home, factory labour was more highly regulated, with its tempo governed by power-driven machines. Workers found this irksome and saw little difference between a factory and a prison.

Mistrust of machinery had a different cause and was not confined to that which was in use in factories. By saving labour, it was feared that machines would produce what later was to become known as "technological unemployment." Widespread protests took place, with outbreaks of rioting and machine wrecking. In 1757 Josiah Tucker complained of "the mistaken notions of the infatuated populace" who consider "inventions as taking the bread out of their mouths, and therefore never fail to break out into riots and insurrections whenever such things are proposed."

In 1780 Dorning Rasbotham, a Manchester magistrate, defended change in the cotton industry:

All improvements in trade by machines do at first produce some difficulties to some particular persons. . . . About ten years ago, when the spinning jennies came up, old persons, children and those who could not easily learn to use their own machines did suffer for a while. . . . What mean those riots and tumults which we saw a few months ago? What mean the petitions to Parliament to suppress or tax the machines? We might just as well ask to have our hands lopped off or our throats cut.

His economic argument was sound. Nevertheless, it is easy to understand why, confronted with protests and disturbances, many manufacturers were content to leave, at least for a time, the setting up of factories and the adoption of power-driven machinery to their more adventurous contemporaries.

Industrial change in one country often has important consequences for the economy of another. This was well illustrated by the developments in the Lancashire cotton industry and their effects on American agriculture. Following the spate of inventions and the spur that it gave to factory production, England's manufacturers began to demand increasing amounts

Eli Whitney
(1765–1825).

of raw cotton. The obvious place to obtain these was from the southern states of America where climatic conditions and a plentiful supply of slave labour favoured the cultivation of the crop. Southerners were eager to satisfy this need, for tobacco was declining in importance as suitable growing areas became worn out; in addition, the export of indigo and rice had

Whitney's cotton gin.

suffered from the recent break with Britain. However, before
the production of raw cotton could be substantially stepped
up, a serious problem had to be overcome. This was the difficulty of separating the cotton seeds from the fibre. Even using
slaves, the process was slow and costly.

Eli Whitney   A temporary solution was found in 1786 with the introduction from the Bahamas of sea island cotton. Because the new
variety had a longer fibre or staple, it was less troublesome to
remove the seeds. Unfortunately, it would thrive only along
the seacoast. Although, for a time, the coastal planters were
able to meet the demand from abroad, some efficient and
speedy way of cleaning the short-staple variety had to be discovered if the rapidly expanding needs of Britain's manufacturers were to be fully met. In 1793 Eli Whitney, a graduate of
Yale who had gone south to become a schoolteacher, came to
the rescue. He invented a machine, known as a gin, which, by
making use of rollers fitted with metal teeth and brushes,
could separate the seeds from short-fibred cotton with speed
32   and efficiency. Whereas before a slave had been able to clean

Unloading bales of cotton from riverboats at New Orleans, 1858.

only about a pound of cotton in one day, by hand-operating
Whitney's gin he could now deal with fifty times that amount.
When driven by water, the machine was capable of handling
a thousand pounds a day.

Whitney's machine, thought by many to be America's first *The cotton gin:*
important agricultural invention, had far-reaching effects. *its effects*
Before long, cotton had supplanted tobacco as the major crop
of the south and had become the nation's largest single export.
Its value was increased still further when uses were found for
the seeds; in 1818 cottonseed oil was developed for lighting
purposes and a few years later, cottonseed cake established
itself as a feed for cattle.

Apart from two brief setbacks,* the production of cotton
was continuous and rapid. Between 1801 and 1805 the average
annual output was 59,600,000 pounds, during the period

* The first of these was in 1808, when a short-lived Embargo Act prevented
American ships from sailing to foreign ports; the second occurred during the war
of 1812–1814.

C

1821–25 it was 209,000,000 pounds, and by 1851–55 it had soared to 1,294,422,800 pounds. At the beginning of the nineteenth century about half of the amount grown was being exported, a figure which steadily rose to four fifths by 1835. Britain was easily the cotton planters' best overseas customer, with France a long way back in second place.

Cotton now dominated the economy of the South. From Georgia and South Carolina its cultivation spread, first into North Carolina and parts of Virginia, then across the Alleghenies into Tennessee. But the advance did not stop there. By 1850 Alabama had become the leading producer and in 1860 this state, along with Louisiana and Mississippi, raised more than half the total output.

Slavery   The effects of this expansion were not limited to the economic life of the nation. There were important social consequences as well. Foremost among these was the stimulus it gave to slavery in the southern states, all the more significant as elsewhere the institution was under attack. George Washington had expressed misgivings about the system, declaring that slaves were a "very troublesome species of property." Thomas Jefferson was another who wished to see slavery abolished. By 1805 abolition had taken place in the North, though trading in slaves was still permitted. Contrary to this liberal movement the number of slaves increased in the South from about 700,000 in 1790 to nearly 4,000,000 in 1860. But even so steep a rise could not satisfy the mounting demand and the average price for a healthy male field hand went from around $800 in 1830 to more than double that figure thirty years later.

Few Southerners were anxious to question the morality of keeping slaves. They, like the textile manufacturers of Lancashire, were content to revel in their new-found prosperity, which they owed to the supremacy of "King Cotton."

CHAPTER THREE

The Age of Steam

"I sell here what all the world desires to have – power!" With these words Matthew Boulton announced that he and his new partner James Watt were now manufacturing steam engines at their factory in Soho, Birmingham.

As long as machines remained small they could be operated by a worker turning a handle or by the movement of his foot on a treadle. But once they became large and more complex, muscle power was no longer sufficient; a greater force was required to make them function. Industrialists felt the growing need for a more effective form of motive power. This, to his evident delight, Boulton was now able to satisfy. The steam engine, which his partner had invented, had shown itself to be both successful and economical to run. By its use steam power could be harnessed to drive a wide range of new machinery, as well as made to perform tasks which had hitherto been beyond the strength of man or beast.

The expansive power of steam had long been known, Hero of Alexandria having designed a steam toy in ancient times. Salomon de Caus, writing in 1615, was probably the first person to point out the practical use which might be made of it, while in 1660 the Marquis of Worcester actually employed steam pressure to raise water into tanks for his fountains. Thirty years later a Frenchman, Denys Papin, demonstrated a machine which operated by alternately heating and cooling steam inside a cylinder. Expanding steam moved a piston upward in the cylinder, while atmospheric pressure forced it down again into the partial vacuum formed as condensation took place.

Early experiments with steam

But none of these early experiments proved of value to industrialists. Some of them tried to solve their power problem by means of the waterwheel. This device had been in use for many centuries, particularly in flour mills and for working the

Water power

35

smelters' bellows and the heavy hammers of ironworks. During the eighteenth century water power began to be employed in the textile industries, first for silk-throwing, then for cotton spinning. It will be recalled that Arkwright's spinning machine was known as a "water frame."

The use of water power, however, had serious disadvantages. It required a factory or ironworks to be located by a swiftly flowing stream or river, a necessity which limited the number of possible sites. The earliest spinning mills, for example, were erected at the foot of the Pennines, where such conditions existed. But given a supply of fast-running water, there were still problems. Waterways are liable to flood; in winter they may become frozen; while in a dry summer their flow will be greatly reduced or may even stop altogether. By interrupting production, any such event could prove a disaster to the manufacturer. Another disadvantage arose from the need to set up factories in hilly areas, for in these regions the roads were usually bad. In consequence, there were difficulties

Boulton and Watt's works at Soho, near Birmingham, 1798.

both over the transportation of raw materials to the site and in the shipment of finished goods.

Drawbacks in the use of the waterwheel prompted men to search for a more reliable means of powering machines. Some, like Thomas Savery, continued to experiment with steam. Savery came from Cornwall, where he learned of the hazards of working copper mines. Foremost among these was the flooding which occurred after a certain depth had been reached. In 1698 he invented a pumping engine that used steam to raise water from underground. Although several of these engines were put into service in Cornish mines, the machine was crude and wasted much energy. *Pumping engines*

In 1708 Thomas Newcomen, a Dartmouth ironmonger, improved upon Savery's pump. His machine consisted of a great timber beam which was connected at one end to a piston, at the other to rods which drew water from the mine through a pipe. The piston moved up and down as steam was first injected into, and then cooled in, the cylinder, the cooling being brought about by means of a spray of water. This type of engine, later improved by John Smeaton, became known as the "Whispering Giant." It has been said that a single Newcomen engine could raise as much water from a mine in two days as twin teams of twenty men and fifty horses, working in shifts, had managed in a week. The machine was much admired, especially by mine owners, who could now sink deeper shafts. Nevertheless, it was far from being perfect, for the method of cooling the steam caused a great loss of heat, making it heavy on fuel and costly to run. It took the scientific genius of James Watt to find a way of removing this defect.

Watt was born at Greenock in Scotland, the son of an architect and shipbuilder. He became fascinated with mechanical devices at a young age and when he had to choose a trade decided to become an instrument maker. For a time he worked at the University of Glasgow, where he met a number of the nation's leading scientists. While there he developed an interest in the problems of steam pressure and when one day he was asked to repair the model of a Newcomen engine which was used for practical purposes in the physics course, he began thinking about how such a machine could be improved. He realized that its chief drawback was the alternate heating and cooling of the cylinder with each stroke of the piston. To over- *James Watt (1736–1819)*

James Watt
(1736–1819).

come this he added a condenser, a second cylinder into which the steam from the main chamber could be drawn off and cooled. This innovation made it possible to keep the temperature of the original cylinder steady and at a high level, with the result that Watt's machine used only a third of the fuel required by Newcomen's engine.

In 1769, after several years of planning and testing, Watt took out a patent for his invention. But he was a poor man troubled with debts. Before his steam engine could go into production he needed someone to finance the enterprise. He found such a person in John Roebuck, a fellow Scot, who was owner of the Carron works. The two men, who had been introduced by a mutual friend at Glasgow University, entered into an agreement. Roebuck promised to build Watt's engine at his works and to make available sufficient capital for him to continue with his experiments; in return he was to receive two thirds of any profits. The partnership, however, was short-lived. Only one engine was produced; known as Beelzebub, this was erected near Edinburgh in 1769. It had many faults, but before Watt had time to remedy these, Roebuck went bankrupt. Watt had no alternative but to seek another backer. But this was no easy quest; months went by and he began to despair of finding a new partner. Just when he had almost given up hope he was approached by Matthew Boulton, with whom he joined forces in 1774. Even now his financial difficulties were not over and many years were to pass before the production of steam engines was to show a profit.

As well as money the construction of steam engines called *The Soho* for a greater precision in metal working than any previously *works* required. The defects in Beelzebub had been largely due to poor workmanship. The prospects at Boulton's Soho works, however, were brighter, for the plant employed many skilled men who were capable of being trained as engineers and fitters to carry out Watt's plans. In the year that the Soho partnership was formed, John Wilkinson, the famous ironmaster, patented his cannon lathe, which could be adapted to produce cylinders that had been bored with accuracy. This was a timely development, for earlier engines had suffered from the leakage of steam caused by badly built cylinders. For years Wilkinson's works at Broseley and Bradley were the sole suppliers of cylinders for Watt's engines.

39

A rotary engine invented by James Watt, 1788.

The Soho factory, sited north of Birmingham, was made up of five buildings holding between six and seven hundred workers. Its products were varied, including metal buttons, chandeliers, ornamental bronzes, vases, and numerous items of ironware. Matthew Boulton, its owner, was a rich man, for, as well as inheriting wealth from his father, he had married an heiress. Though he might well have retired into a life of leisure, he preferred the world of industry and was never happier than when he was working on some new scheme to expand his interests. Therefore it was with enthusiasm that he joined with Watt in developing the steam engine.

Rotary engines The partnership seemed secured in 1775 when Watt obtained a twenty-five-year extension of his patent. This gave the new firm of Boulton and Watt the sole right to erect and control the operation of steam engines. Even so, production was for a time slow and by 1781 only about fifty engines had been made. One reason for this was the limited uses to which they could be put; these were mainly for pumping or blowing blast furnaces. As a result, Watt tried to devise a way of converting the to-and-fro action into a rotary movement. Success came in 1781. By making use of a "sun and planet" system,

40

whereby power was transmitted from the piston to a beam, and from the beam to a shaft, he produced an engine which could be made to drive a much wider variety of machines. By the end of the century nearly a hundred of these rotary engines were already at work in cotton mills.

During the Industrial Revolution Britain became the lead- *The iron* ing metalworking country in the world. Progress in her iron *industry* industry owed much to the development of power production, for steam pressure placed such a severe strain on machines that wood was no longer a satisfactory material from which to make them. Another stimulus was the lengthy war with France and its demands for large quantities of munitions.

The iron industry was divided into two parts; on the one hand there were the mining and smelting branches, on the other the branches that were concerned with working the metal into manufactured articles. At the beginning of the eighteenth century the industry was in a hazardous condition, particularly in the primary stages, and there was little to indicate the prosperity which lay ahead. The chief cause of the existing stagnation was the difficulty in smelting iron. This process involves the heating of the ore until the metal which it holds melts and runs off, freed from most of its impurities. Traditionally, iron smelters had made use of charcoal as fuel in their blast furnaces, which were dispersed throughout the whole of Britain. By 1700, however, many of the great woods and forests of the past had dwindled in size; there was a scarcity of suitable timber for charcoal, with the result that its cost had risen astronomically. If the nation's iron industry was to survive some alternative fuel had to be found.

During the seventeenth century protests had been voiced against the "waste and destruction of the woods" perpetrated by the smelters. Some people feared that the growing shortage of timber would adversely affect the Royal Navy's shipbuilding programme. In 1677 Andrew Yarranton showed the hostility felt towards the industry when he wrote: "It were well if there were no ironworks in England, and it was better when no iron was made in England, and the ironworks destroy all the woods."

Early attempts were made to substitute coal for charcoal in *Coal for* the smelting process – Dud Dudley carried out such an experi- *charcoal* ment in 1619 – but these proved unsuccessful, for the sul- 41 phurous fumes that coal gave off ruined the quality of the metal. It was left to the first Abraham Darby to find the way. He had the idea of using coal which had first been reduced to coke. The exact date of the discovery is not certain, but it must have been soon after he founded the famous Darby ironworks at Coalbrooksdale, Shropshire, in 1709. Many years later, in a letter to a friend, his son's wife, Abiah, told how her father-in-law "first tried with raw coal as it came out of the mines, but it did not answer." Undismayed he "had the coal coked into cinder, as is done for drying malt, and it then succeeded to his satisfaction."

Coke smelting was slow to spread to other parts of Britain. It seems likely that the Darbys themselves took steps to guard their process, confining it within the family and a small circle of friends. Its introduction was also delayed by the fact that coke had to be heated to a greater temperature than charcoal if no ore was to be left unsmelted. This meant that a stronger blast had to be used for the furnaces. The second Abraham

An open hearth iron foundry, 1802.

Darby obtained more power by using a Newcomen engine to pump a better head of water for the wheel that worked his bellows. A big improvement came in 1761 when John Smeaton invented a blowing apparatus which consisted of cylindrical air pumps whose pistons could be worked either by a waterwheel or by a steam engine. A further advance was made in 1828. J. B. Neilson, a Scot, discovered that by using waste heat from the furnace he could replace the former cold blast with a hot one, thereby considerably reducing his coke bill.

The Coalbrookdale process made pig, or cast, iron which *Wrought iron* was hard and brittle. This was because of its high carbon content. To obtain a more pliable metal, the pig iron had to be heated, hammered, and reheated several times at the forge in order to remove some of the carbon, but it was a lengthy business and only moderately successful. A more efficient method of producing malleable iron was needed.

During the eighteenth century experiments were undertaken with reverberating furnaces in which the metal and fuel were kept apart. By playing flames from above onto the pig iron it was hoped to burn off more of the impurities. The brothers George and Thomas Cranage, who worked for the Darbys, were the first to develop a reverberating system which was commercially viable and the method was introduced at Coalbrookdale in 1766.

It was the invention of *puddling*, however, which opened the way for a large-scale production of wrought iron. Henry Cort, a contractor to the Admiralty, and Peter Onions, a foreman in an iron mill in South Wales, did not know each other, yet within a few months in 1784 both had arrived at the same solution for removing the carbonic impurities from pig iron. Unfairly perhaps, history has tended to assign the credit to Cort, who certainly did more to publicize the revolutionary implications of the puddling process. Both men discovered that by mixing iron oxides with the heated pig iron, which were then stirred or puddled together with long hooks called clinker bars, the oxygen in the oxides could be made to combine with the unwanted carbon. The result was a metal low in carbon that was less brittle. Henry Cort also invented a rolling mill which converted the lumps of wrought iron into bars and plates suitable for many new uses in the manufacturing branches of the industry.

So long as Britain's smelters had been unable to satisfy the demand of iron manufacturers in centres like Birmingham, Sheffield and Dudley, the latter were compelled to pay a high price for imports of pig and wrought iron from Sweden and Russia. Technological improvements such as coke smelting and puddling now made this unnecessary. The increase in home production is most dramatically illustrated by the works at Coalbrookdale where, in 1717, about five hundred tons of pig iron were produced, against thirteen or fourteen thousand tons a year by the end of the century. Throughout the industry as a whole output rose from sixty-eight thousand tons in 1788 to nearly four times that amount twenty years later.

But this was not the only effect of technical change. Another was on the siting of the industry, which was now attracted to the coalfields. The use of coal for smelting meant that it was more economical to build furnaces where the fuel was mined. In addition, a need to be near coal was created by the growing importance of steam power in the production of iron.

John Wilkinson   Improvements were also introduced into the manufacturing branches for whom Cort's rolling mill made it possible to produce bars and sheets of iron to a required length, thickness, and strength. Power-driven machines for cutting, turning, and drilling metal were developed. John Wilkinson was outstanding among a group of men who became "mad" about iron, seeing limitless possibilities for its use. In 1779 he built an iron bridge across the Severn River and eight years later astonished people by successfully launching a boat made of iron plates. He manufactured cast-iron pipes, of value in the construction of better water systems for towns, and supplied forty miles of these to the city of Paris alone. An iron chapel, built for the Methodists of Bradley, was another of his ideas. Wilkinson dreamed of a time when, supplanting other materials, iron would be used for the making of houses and roads. When this remarkable man died in 1805, he was buried, as was only right and proper, in an iron coffin.

Coal   The coal industry was already well established in Britain by the beginning of the eighteenth century. Mining took place in several areas including Yorkshire, Derbyshire, Nottinghamshire, South Lancashire, and the West Midlands, but it was along the valley of the Tyne that the largest centre of production was to be found. By 1725 there were thirty thousand men

44

At the pit-head of a coal mine in 1839.

working in the Tyneside collieries, much of their output being shipped to London by coastal vessels. The use of coal for domestic purposes was well known in early Tudor times, but it was not until the reign of Elizabeth I that it began to be employed in the nation's industries. With the growing timber shortage an increasing number of these turned to coal as an alternative fuel. Among manufacturers to take this step were some who made bricks, dyes, glass, alum, soap, and starch, or who were engaged in sugar refining and brewing.

With the development of coke smelting and the growing use of steam power, new forces were at work to stimulate the production of coal. But before any major expansion could take place mining had to be made safer. Water was a constant enemy of the worker underground, but first by means of Newcomen's steam pump, then by making use of Watt's engine, much was done to improve drainage. There was also the threat from poisonous gases, *chokedamp*, or carbonic acid gas, being especially troublesome. The construction of ventilation shafts to ensure a circulation of air went part of the way toward removing the danger of suffocation. Even more deadly was marsh gas, known to miners as *firedamp*; this exploded without warning when it came into contact with the naked flame of the miner's candle and was the cause of frequent disasters. It was not until the introduction of safety lamps, the most successful of which was invented by Sir Humphry Davy in

Mining hazards

45

1815, that the number of explosions was significantly reduced. Finally, there was always the risk of a cave-in, though this hazard was somewhat lessened after 1810 when wooden pit props began to be used to support roofs.

But these improvements were a mixed blessing for the miner as they encouraged colliery owners to sink deeper shafts and work seams at a more dangerous level. Therefore, in spite of such safety measures, the number of accidents remained high.

Moving the coal A second set of problems which had to be solved by the mining industry related to the movement of coal, a heavy and bulky material. There was the difficulty of bringing the coal to the surface. So long as pits remained shallow this could be managed by men and women, who climbed ladders with baskets of coal strapped to their backs. Once mines became deeper, some other means had to be found, not only of raising the coal, but for transporting the miners up and down the shafts as well. Winding machines provided the answer. At first these were worked by horses but, as the eighteenth century drew to a close, steam engines took over.

Waterways were the cheapest and easiest routes along which to transport coal once it was on the surface, but the nearest of these was often several miles from the pit head. As early as the seventeenth century wooden tracks had been laid from many a pit to some nearby river so that coal could be more easily taken to it in horse-drawn wagons. After 1767 iron railroads were gradually introduced, making links not only with natural waterways but also with newly built canals.

Railways Of all the machines to come out of the Industrial Revolution none has captured the public imagination more than the locomotive. It was to revolutionize transportation and prove of incalculable value to manufacturers throughout the world. Yet, originally, the locomotive had been designed for use within the mining industry.

George Stephenson, the most famous of the railway pioneers, worked as a colliery engineman near Newcastle. Among his early accomplishments was the invention of a miner's safety lamp, which he tested in a gas-polluted mine at considerable risk to his life. Impressed by the *Puffing Billy*, which William Hedley had just built for use at a neighbouring colliery, Stephenson persuaded his employer to let him construct a locomotive. The result was the *Blucher*, completed in 1814. A few years later he became engineer to the company formed to construct a railway between Stockton and Darlington. When the line opened in 1825, Stephenson's engine *Locomotion* pulled a train which was composed of twenty-one passenger wagons and twelve trucks of coal. In consequence of the cheaper transportation costs, the price of coal at Darlington fell from 18 shillings to 8 shillings a ton.

In spite of the many technical advances made within the coal industry, the actual business of coal-getting remained little changed. There was no mechanical revolution to ease the plight of the miner, for whom working conditions were harsh and exhausting. Coal continued to be dug by hand and, though ponies were used in some pits after 1700, in most it was still taken from where it was cut to the bottom of the shaft by human labour. To make matters worse, as the industry ex-

*Working
conditions*

Locomotives under construction at a railway works, 1835.

panded, a greater use was made of women and children below ground.

It is not surprising to learn that in most mines relationships between the owners and the miners were bad. The capitalists who owned the collieries showed little concern for the well-being of their employees. They too faced risks which, in their eyes, were far greater than those of the workers underground. Mining was a costly, chancy undertaking, in which profits could all too easily turn to losses. At a time when the location of seams was largely a matter of trial and error, pits often ran out of coal and had to be closed. Humanitarian feelings were a luxury which many owners felt they could not afford.

The miners, for their part, were resentful of the fact that when injured they could claim no compensation from employers. In addition, they were bitter about the terms of service, especially those in the Midlands, where a butty system operated. Under this system the miners were hired by a middleman known as a butty. It was to him that the colliery owner, relieved of the trouble of having to find his own workers, made payment. It was from the butty that the miners received their wages. Many protested, not without cause, that the man who hired them was getting rich at their expense.

Without an increase in coal production the development of steam power would not have been possible. It is sad to reflect that industrial progress was purchased at so high a price in human suffering and misery – that it was paid for with the broken bodies of countless men, women, and children who laboured in a dungeonlike world underground.

CHAPTER FOUR

Cheap and Easy Transportation

For hundreds of years the safest way of sending goods from *Hazardous*
one part of Britain to another was by packhorse. Strings of as *travel*
many as forty horses were a common sight on the country
roads, the leading animal carrying a bell to give warning to
other travellers to move aside. However, owing to the bad
condition of most roads, transportation by this method was
very slow. Under an Act of 1555 the inhabitants of each parish
had been made responsible for the repair and upkeep of the
highways within their district, but the system did not work
well and many roads were unusable for months at a time. In
wet weather they became quagmires; when it was dry they
were rutted and full of deep holes. Newspapers in the eighteenth century contained many accounts of the hazards which
travellers had to face. For example, in 1769 *The Ipswich Journal*
told of a man who, having been thrown from his horse, fell into
a ditch where he was suffocated by mud and filth. There were
stories of coaches overturned many times while making a
single journey. Conditions were little better in the cities, and
London, in particular, was notorious for the deplorable state
of its streets.

Although some traders used carts or wagons instead of *A complaint*
packhorses, the advantage of being able to carry more goods *to Parliament*
was offset by the extra risks encountered by these heavy
vehicles. Something had to be done to improve road surfaces.

Early in the eighteenth century a number of "merchants,
tradesmen and other inhabitants living in or near the road
from Liverpool to Prescott" complained to Parliament:

That the Road . . . is very much used in the carriage of coals (to
Liverpool and also from Liverpool) to the towns of Wigan, Bolton,
Rochdale, Warrington and Manchester, and to the counties of
York, Derby and other eastern parts of the kingdom, in the carriage
of wool, cotton, malt, and all other merchants goods; whereby 49

D

several parts of the said road are so very deep, and other parts so narrow, that coaches, wagons, and other wheel carriages cannot pass through the same; nor can the same be effectively repaired and enlarged, without some further provision be made for that purpose.

In reply Parliament agreed to the formation of a turnpike trust.

Turnpike trusts   Here was a way to get better roads. The first turnpike trust had been set up in 1663 and by the following century there were already several similar bodies established. Each was entrusted by Act of Parliament to repair and keep in order a particular stretch of road. Tolls could be charged to pay for the work, these being collected at gates or turnpikes erected every few miles. Turnpike companies were also formed in the United States, though not until a later date; the first one built a road from Philadelphia to Lancaster, Pennsylvania, between 1792 and 1794. In America, however, the word "turnpike" usually referred to the road itself and not, as in Britain, to one of its tollgates.

The system flourished in Britain, for men with capital were eager to form trusts because they promised a fruitful investment. As for traders and other travellers, most agreed with Daniel Defoe that "the benefit of a good road abundantly" made amends for "that little charge" they were asked to pay at the turnpikes.

Their drawbacks   The turnpike system was much better than leaving the roads in the care of the parishes, but it fell far short of providing a cheap and easy means of transportation. Trusts were often inefficiently administered and at times those who ran them had self-interest, rather than the public welfare, at heart. As most companies controlled relatively short stretches of road they did nothing to establish a network of trunk roads. This failure partly accounts for the decline in road traffic after 1830 when railways came on the scene. Had the trusts amalgamated, as did the railway companies, the story might have been very different.

Road making   The techniques of road making had been virtually ignored since the time of the Romans, and even when the trusts took over they continued the old practice of filling in ruts and holes. As more and heavier vehicles were attracted to the turnpike

roads the problem of maintaining them in good order became

An English stage wagon, 1815. Drawn by eight horses this broad-wheeled vehicle was very slow and was mainly used to carry goods long distances over rough roads.

acute. After 1760 a new class of road engineers began to work out ways of constructing roads which had firm foundations, strong surfaces, and were well drained. One was John Metcalfe who, though blind since the age of six, was responsible for linking the industrial areas of Yorkshire and Lancashire by means of a highway from Huddersfield to Manchester. A second, Thomas Telford, also gained a reputation for canal and bridge building; probably his greatest achievement was the Menai Suspension Bridge which connected the mainland of Wales to the island of Anglesey. Among the roads that he improved was one from Carlisle to Glasgow and another from Shrewsbury to Holyhead.

The most outstanding of these engineers was John Mac-adam. His method of making a road was very different from that of his rivals, or indeed from the way that those other great road builders, the Romans, had used nearly two thousand years before. Unlike them he dispensed with a thick founda-tion, setting his road straight onto the "native soil." Layers of stones were built up, the components of which became smaller 51

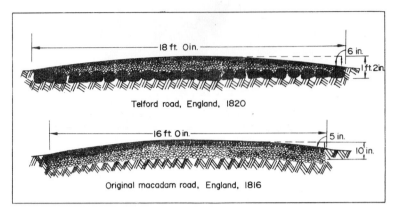

18 ft. 0 in.

6 in.

1 ft. 2 in.

Telford road, England, 1820

16 ft. 0 in.

5 in.

10 in.

Original macadam road, England, 1816

Cross sections of roads as constructed by (a) Telford and (b) Macadam.

the nearer to the surface they were placed. Vehicles using the highway pressed the smaller stones between the larger ones, thereby making a firm and watertight surface. At first people laughed at his ideas but gradually "macadamized" roads appeared in many parts of the country. On October 8, 1824, *The Times* reported:

Yesterday the workmen began to Macadamize the wide roadway from Charing Cross to Parliament Square. . . . The great granite stones are broke into small pieces as soon as they are taken up, and thus, as rapidly as the way is cleared the materials are ready for commencement of the Macadamizing system.

Better roads meant faster travel for passengers and by 1836 there were more than three thousand coaches on British roads, many maintaining speeds of ten miles an hour. Journeys which had once taken days were now covered in a few hours. The effects on goods vehicles, however, were less striking. Although the number of carriers increased, especially in the northern industrial districts, the pace at which they operated remained slow; in 1835, for example, the famous firm of Pickfords allowed eight hours for a wagon to make the journey of sixteen miles between Sheffield and Castleton. At the same time, their charges were high, particularly for heavy commodities. It was to obtain a cheaper means of moving bulky materials like coal, iron, and clay that attempts were made to improve the country's waterways.

52

At first improvers concentrated on the navigation of exist- *Canals*
ing rivers, which were deepened and made wider. But the
benefits from these schemes were limited and during the
second half of the eighteenth century attentions turned to the
construction of artificial waterways. Before long Britain was
in the throes of a canal-building boom.

It was James Brindley who was largely responsible for this
new development. Although illiterate, he possessed an outstanding mechanical skill and when the Duke of Bridgewater
decided to build a canal from his mines at Worsley to the town
of Manchester, a distance of about seven miles, Brindley was
put in charge of the undertaking. The route lay across uneven
country and the Duke thought that it would be necessary to
build a series of locks along the canal. Brindley suggested a
better way. He would maintain the water level by cutting
tunnels through high ground and constructing embankments
where the land was low. The canal, which was opened in 1761,
was a great success. Reports claimed that it had the effect of
halving the price of coal at Manchester.

Even more important, it encouraged the Duke of Bridge- *Brindley's*
water and other magnates to finance similar schemes else- *plan*
where. Josiah Wedgwood, the famous Staffordshire pottery
manufacturer, for example, employed Brindley to build the
Grand Trunk Canal linking the Trent and Mersey rivers.
Brindley died from overwork before this enterprise was completed, but by this time he had mapped out plans for a network
of canals to cover the whole country. By 1830 his dream had
been realized and more than a hundred canals, totalling nearly
two thousand miles, were in operation.

Canals were of considerable value to both mining and manu- *Its effects*
facturing districts. Heavy china clay could now be brought
from Cornwall to the Staffordshire potteries at a saving of £2
a ton, while the cheaper movement of coal benefited all industries that used steam power. Industry also gained from the
lower costs of transporting building materials needed both for
the construction of factories and for the houses of the workers.
Canals extended industrial development by opening up new
sites; manufacturers were encouraged to move outside the
towns and locate their mills and workshops along the waterways where land was cheaper.

At the very height of their success canals began to be challenged by the railways, which soon showed that they could carry goods more quickly and at low costs. As a result a declining use was made of the nation's waterway system as the nineteenth century wore on. It is not without irony that the engineers who now laid mile after mile of railroads, thereby contributing to the downfall of the canals, were indebted to men like Brindley and Telford for many of the techniques which they employed.

Brittle rails   We have already seen how the earliest railroads were laid to connect collieries to nearby rivers and canals. The tracks were made of wood, metal not being used until after 1767, when Richard Reynolds, working at Coalbrookdale, cast the first iron rails. Although the new tracks did not wear out as quickly as wooden ones, their value was reduced by the fact that they kept breaking. The invention of the steam locomotive made their weakness a serious problem, for they now had to withstand a weight which was greater than that of any wagon. Watt's patents had expired in 1799 and this freed the way for others to explore methods of using steam power to propel a vehicle. Almost at once a Cornishman named Richard Trevithick produced a locomotive that would run on rails. Unfortunately attempts to demonstrate his invention were a failure; though the engine worked well, the rails proved too weak to support the locomotive. But for this, Trevithick, rather than George Stephenson, might have been acclaimed as "the father of the steam locomotive." Luckily for Stephenson, by the time that he came to start work on the "Stockton and Darlington Rail Way" in 1821, John Birkinshaw of Bedlington Ironworks in Northumberland had just discovered a way of making wrought-iron rails. Less brittle than those of cast iron, the new rails could safely be made of much greater length. At first they weighed seventeen pounds to the yard, but by 1850 this had risen to eighty pounds.

Liverpool   The Stockton and Darlington line, opened in 1825, was
to Manchester   Britain's first real railway. Soon plans were being drawn up
by rail   for a more ambitious venture, a track to connect the two great industrial centres of Liverpool and Manchester. Parliament,

(*Opposite*) The Rainhill Trials, 1829: three of the locomotives that competed.

1829.

GRAND COMPETITION

OF

LOCOMOTIVES

ON THE

LIVERPOOL & MANCHESTER RAILWAY.

STIPULATIONS & CONDITIONS

ON WHICH THE DIRECTORS OF THE LIVERPOOL AND MANCHESTER RAILWAY OFFER A PREMIUM OF £500 FOR THE MOST IMPROVED LOCOMOTIVE ENGINE.

I.

The said Engine must "effectually consume its own smoke," according to the provisions of the Railway Act, 7th Geo. IV.

II.

The Engine, if it weighs Six Tons, must be capable of drawing after it, day by day, on a well-constructed Railway, on a level plane, a Train of Carriages of the gross weight of Twenty Tons, including the Tender and Water Tank, at the rate of Ten Miles per Hour, with a pressure of steam in the boiler not exceeding Fifty Pounds on the square inch.

III.

There must be Two Safety Valves, one of which must be completely out of the reach or control of the Engine-man, and neither of which must be fastened down while the Engine is working.

IV.

The Engine and Boiler must be supported on Springs, and rest on Six Wheels; and the height from the ground to the top of the Chimney must not exceed Fifteen Feet.

V.

The weight of the Machine, WITH ITS COMPLEMENT OF WATER in the Boiler, must, at most, not exceed Six Tons, and a Machine of less weight will be preferred if it draw AFTER it a PROPORTIONATE weight; and if the weight of the Engine, &c., do not exceed FIVE TONS, then the gross weight to be drawn need not exceed Fifteen Tons; and in that proportion for Machines of still smaller weight — provided that the Engine, &c., shall still be on six wheels, unless the weight (as above) be reduced to Four Tons and a Half, or under, in which case the Boiler, &c., may be placed on four wheels. And the Company shall be at liberty to put the Boiler, Fire Tube, Cylinders, &c., to the test of a pressure of water not exceeding 150 Pounds per square inch, without being answerable for any damage the Machine may receive in consequence.

VI.

There must be a Mercurial Gauge affixed to the Machine, with Index Rod, showing the Steam Pressure above 45 Pounds per square inch; and constructed to blow out a Pressure of 60 Pounds per inch.

VII.

The Engine to be delivered complete for trial, at the Liverpool end of the Railway, not later than the 1st of October next.

VIII.

The price of the Engine which may be accepted, not to exceed £550, delivered on the Railway; and any Engine not approved to be taken back by the Owner.

N.B.—The Railway Company will provide the ENGINE TENDER with a supply of Water and Fuel, for the experiment. The distance within the Rails is four feet eight inches and a half.

THE LOCOMOTIVE STEAM ENGINES,

WHICH COMPETED FOR THE PRIZE OF £500 OFFERED BY THE DIRECTORS OF THE LIVERPOOL AND MANCHESTER RAILWAY COMPANY.

DRAWN TO A SCALE ¼ INCH TO A FOOT.

THE "ROCKET" OF Mr. ROBT. STEPHENSON OF NEWCASTLE,

WHICH DRAWING A LOAD EQUIVALENT TO THREE TIMES ITS WEIGHT TRAVELLED AT THE RATE OF 12½ MILES AN HOUR, AND WITH A CARRIAGE & PASSENGERS AT THE RATE OF 24 MILES. COST PER MILE FOR FUEL ABOUT THREE HALF PENCE.

THE "NOVELTY" OF MESSRS. BRAITHWAITE & ERRICSSON OF LONDON,

WHICH DRAWING A LOAD EQUIVALENT TO THREE TIMES ITS WEIGHT TRAVELLED AT THE RATE OF 20¾ MILES AN HOUR, AND WITH A CARRIAGE & PASSENGERS AT THE RATE OF 32 MILES. COST PER MILE FOR FUEL ABOUT ONE HALFPENNY.

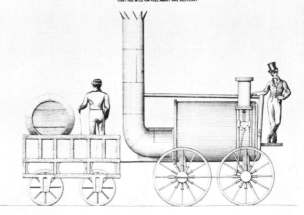

THE "SANSPAREIL" OF Mr. HACKWORTH OF DARLINGTON,

WHICH DRAWING A LOAD EQUIVALENT TO THREE TIMES ITS WEIGHT TRAVELLED AT THE RATE OF 12½ MILES AN HOUR. COST FOR FUEL PER MILE ABOUT TWO PENCE.

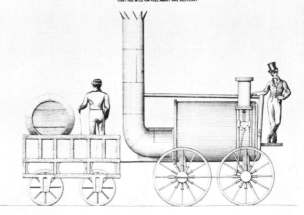

The Liverpool and Manchester Railway: the differences between First and Second Class travel.

however, was reluctant to give its consent to the scheme. There were many powerful interests at work who were anxious to prevent the enterprise. These included canal proprietors and the owners of stagecoach lines, who feared the competition of the railways, and landowners who believed that livestock would be terrorized by the noise and fiery appearance of the engines. After much delay Parliament gave its approval and the project got under way. But though defeated this time, the opponents of the railway were not finished. For years ahead there were many such men who never missed a chance of attacking the railway companies or of sabotaging their undertakings.

Stephenson was placed in charge of the line's construction, a difficult operation for there were many obstacles to overcome, not least of which was the crossing of Chat Moss, a treacherous bog. Fifty-eight bridges had to be built along its route. The famous Rainhill Trials offered a prize worth £500 to the inventor of a locomotive "which should be a decided improvement on those now in use as respects the consumption of coke, increased, adequate power, and moderate weight." The contest, as most people know, was won by

Stephenson's *Rocket*; what is perhaps less well known is the fact that it was George's son, Robert, who was mainly responsible for the design and construction of the winning entry.

The Liverpool and Manchester railway was opened in 1830 *Railway mania* and in its first year made twice the profit that had been expected. The country was poised for a railway boom which was to make the earlier mania for canals pale into insignificance. By 1838 nearly five hundred miles of track had been built; this included a line joining London and Birmingham. Within five years the total mileage had risen to 1,900 and by 1850 had soared to 6,600.

Other countries were swift to follow Britain's example. *In other* France had its first railway in 1832, while Germany and *countries* Belgium started lines three years later. In America the first attempt to run a steam locomotive was made in 1829 on the Carbondale and Honedale railroad, but it was a failure, the *Stourbridge Lion*, which had been brought from England, proving too heavy for the rails. The previous year, on July 4, construction had begun on the Baltimore and Ohio railway, but it was not until 1830 that the promoters were finally convinced that the trains should be pulled by steam rather than horse power. Then, as the company building the Liverpool and Manchester line had done in England, they held a competition to find a suitable locomotive. The first prize of $4,000 was won by a watchmaker named Phineas Davis, whose *York* became the prototype for a whole fleet of engines.

Advantages   The railways soon demonstrated that they could offer a faster means of transportation than either the roads or the canals. As early as the 1830's trains were averaging more than twenty-five miles an hour. Within a few years freight charges had been cut, in some cases to less than half those formerly demanded by road carriers. Another advantage of the railways was their ability to surmount natural barriers, thereby reducing the distance which had to be travelled. Stephenson laid his track straight across the Chat Moss bog. Other railway engineers drove great tunnels through hills and mountains. An early example was the Kilsby Tunnel, near Rugby, during the construction of which twenty-six men lost their lives. Another, completed in 1845, was the Woodhead Tunnel on the Sheffield and Manchester line; this was over three miles in length. Rail travel was also more reliable, for it was safer than journeying by road or waterway and less subject to interruption by bad weather.

The coming of the railways: a contemporary comment on what this meant for coach operators.

Kilsby Tunnel, during the construction of which twenty-six men died, 1837.

By 1850 nearly all the main lines which today form England's railway system had been completed or were under construction. These trunk routes had been made possible by the amalgamation movement during the past decade. Like the turnpike trusts and canal companies, most of the early railway companies operated over distances which were often no more than a few miles in length. This was unsatisfactory. The need to change trains, perhaps several times on a long journey, caused delays. The public, therefore, welcomed the consolidation of railways which took place during the 1840's, while the companies saw amalgamation as a means of reducing their operating costs. No person did more to foster this movement than George Hudson; his greatest achievement was the formation of the Midland Railway by the fusion of three companies, all of which had lines running into Derby.

Amalgamation highlighted the need of Britain's railways for a uniform gauge, or distance separating a pair of tracks. Several gauges had been tried by the early companies, though in the north a gauge of 4 feet 8½ inches, the "narrow gauge" used by George Stephenson, had gradually been accepted as standard. However in the south there were some who favoured a gauge of 7 feet which, it was claimed, would permit faster, smoother, and safer travel. The great advocate of the "broad gauge" was Isambard Kingdom Brunel, a brilliant engineer who, in 1833, joined what was to become the Great Western Railway. To facilitate further amalgamations Parliament, in 1846, decided the issue, choosing the narrow gauge for the nation's railways. In the United States there were similar difficulties over the establishment of a standard gauge. For a time more than twenty different gauges, ranging from 3 to 6 feet, were in use in various parts of the country. It was not until the 1870's that agreement was reached, as in Britain, on a gauge of 4 feet 8½ inches. This has become the standard in many other countries. In the Soviet Union, however, the gauge is 5 feet, a legacy from Czarist times when the state chose a gauge which was different from that of any of her neighbours as a safeguard from an invasion by railway-borne troops.

These developments were accompanied by important changes in sea travel. Ships appeared made of iron instead of
wood and steam began to replace wind and sail as the means of

The London to Greenwich Railway as seen from the Surrey Canal.

propulsion. However, the progress of these innovations was slow. Though both were introduced in the 1780's, Wilkinson's iron boat and a steamer designed by the British engineer William Symington being launched within a year of each other, the wooden sailing ship remained the most common vessel afloat on the high seas until the second half of the following century.

Among those who met Symington and took a trip on one of his steamers was a young American painter named Robert Fulton. He at once saw the commercial possibilities of using such craft on the great wide rivers of his own country. Anxious to exploit these, he returned home and began building the *Clermont*, which, in 1807, became the first steamship to carry passengers and goods by making a memorable voyage up the Hudson River from New York to Albany. Within five years similar vessels were at work on the Mississippi.

In 1819 the *Savannah*, built in New York, crossed the Atlantic equipped with steam and sail, but though the voyage lasted twenty-seven days, she was under steam only for about

A steam-powered ship of the British navy, 1845.

eighty hours. The first all-steam crossing was made in 1833 by the Canadian *Royal William*. British steamships began to ply the Atlantic in 1838 when the *Sirius* sailed from London to New York in seventeen days. Two years later *Britannia*, a wooden vessel built on the Clyde for Samuel Cunard, was the first steamship to carry mail from Britain to North America. Charles Dickens was among those who travelled on her shortly after she went into service, and he described the trip in his *American Notes* (1842). It was not until 1856, however, that the Cunard Line built a steamship that was made of iron.

The Industrial Revolution created the need for a more efficient system of transportation. In turn, it made such a system possible, providing through the mining and metallurgical industries the materials, the tools, and many of the techniques used by those who carried out the various improvements outlined in this chapter.

CHAPTER FIVE

Masters and Men

The Industrial Revolution did not create capitalism; this had existed for centuries. Nor was it responsible for first setting labourer against employer. What did happen after 1750 was a marked growth in the capitalistic organization of industry, as a result of which increasing numbers of people became involved in a new kind of economic relationship. Before long two new classes had taken shape, the one composed of industrial capitalists, the other of the workers that they employed.

With few exceptions, notably Boulton, Watt, and Wedgwood, the early industrial capitalists were coarse, uncultured men. Their origins were varied. A number had agricultural backgrounds. Joshua Fielden and the Peels, for example, were born into farming families where work on the land was combined with hand-loom weaving. David Dale, another prominent member of the cotton trade, tended cattle as a boy in Scotland. Most of the ironmasters, on the other hand, had close links with the metal industries from childhood. Ambrose Crowley started his working life in an ironmonger's shop; the first Abraham Darby was trained as a locksmith; and John Roebuck was the son of a Sheffield manufacturer. Other industrialists had origins that showed little connection with their later activities: John Horrocks was a stonecutter by trade; Richard Arkwright was a barber; and Robert Owen found an early livelihood as a linen draper's assistant.

Industrial capitalists

Few of these men had any real inventive flair. They owed success to their organizing ability and the skill with which they could manage finance and control labour. Ruthless, tough, they had little time for niceties in the running of their works. Driving themselves hard, they expected those that they employed to do the same. Compassion was lacking from their make-up: to them the workers were "hands," who could be more easily replaced than the costly machines they operated. There were 63 a few exceptions. Robert Owen, outstanding among these, was a model factory owner who housed and cared for the workers at his New Lanark mill in a manner far ahead of the times. He complained that all too often "the employer regards the employed as mere instruments of gain."

"They are petty monarchs"

What did the workers think of these "captains of industry"? In 1818 a certain journeyman cotton spinner had this to say about the employers in his trade:

> With very few exceptions, they are a set of men . . . without education or address, except so much as they have acquired by their intercourse with the little world of merchants on the exchange at Manchester; but to counterbalance that deficiency, they give you enough of appearances by an ostentatious display of elegant mansions, equipages, liveries, parks, hunters, hounds, etc., which they take care to show off to the merchant stranger in the most pompous manner. Indeed their houses are gorgeous palaces, far surpassing in bulk and extent the neat charming retreats you see round London . . . but the chaste observer of the beauties of nature and art combined will observe a woeful deficiency of taste. . . . They are literally petty monarchs, absolute and despotic, in their own particular districts; and to support all this, their whole time is occupied in contriving how to get the greatest quantity of work turned off with the least expense. . . . They are ignorant, proud, and tyrannical.

From Mary Barton

The age-old division of society into rich and poor took on a new significance during the Industrial Revolution. Many people shared the view of Benjamin Disraeli, expressed in his novel *Sybil* (1845), and saw Britain as a land that was now divided into "two nations," the haves and the have-nots. Another English novelist, Mrs. Elizabeth Gaskell, gave a graphic illustration of this social cleavage in *Mary Barton* (1848):

> At all times it is a bewildering thing to the poor weaver to see his employer removing from house to house, each one grander than the last, till he ends in building one more magnificent than all, or withdraws his money from the concern, or sells his mill to buy an estate in the country, while all the time the weaver, who thinks he and his fellows are the real makers of this wealth, is struggling on for bread for their children, through their vicissitudes of lowered wages, short hours, fewer hands employed, etc.
>
> And when he knows trade is bad, and could understand (at least

partially) that there are not buyers enough in the market to pur-chase the goods already made, and consequently that there is no demand for more; when he would bear and endure much without complaining, could he also see his employers were bearing their share; he is, I say, bewildered and (to use his own words) "aggra-vated" to see that all goes on just as usual with the mill-owners. Large houses are still occupied, while spinners' and weavers' cottages stand empty, because the families that once occupied them are obliged to live in rooms and cellars.

During the later part of the eighteenth century new econo- *Laissez-faire* mic theories gained ground. These supported industrialists in their growing struggle against workers and warned against the dangers of making concessions over wages and hours. The doctrine of laissez-faire, explained by Adam Smith in *The Wealth of Nations* (1776), stressed the importance of self-interest. One should not speak to a manufacturer about humanity, Smith said, but address his attention to the per-sonal advantages which were to be derived from trade. Government had a negative part to play – the less it interfered in economic matters the better. Laws which regulated indus-try or restricted commerce were to be abolished. Prosperity would come only when each man was free to pursue his own interest. Acceptance of such a policy favoured the employers for it prevented Parliament from taking steps to shorten work-ing hours in factories and mines or improve conditions. In 1833 when Lord Ashley tried to reduce the time that a child might labour each day in a textile mill, he was greeted with a barrage of abuse from manufacturers; fearing that such a measure would ruin them, his opponents accused Ashley of attempting to undermine the whole structure of British industry.

Employers got further support from the writings of Thomas *Prophets of* Malthus and David Ricardo, of whom it has been said that *despair* they made economics a "dismal science." Malthus pointed out that the population of a country increases at a more rapid rate than the production of food. This was an alarming situa-tion. But fortunately Nature had a solution. By means of poverty, wars, famine, and diseases she maintained a balance between consumers and the available supply of food. Any improvements which employers made in working conditions, therefore, would only obstruct Nature in her process. Malthus 65

E

subsequently modified this gloomy picture by admitting that human beings could themselves operate checks; they could remain celibate, marry later in life, or restrict the size of their families. Nevertheless, it still followed that nothing should be done to ease the lot of the poor, for higher wages or charity would only tempt them to have more children.

As for Ricardo, he too was concerned with "natural laws" from which there was no escape. Workers, he said, would always tend to earn just enough money to live on and no more. Wage increases were no lasting gain; encouraging those who received them to breed could lead only to a situation in which there were more workers than available jobs. By the iron law of wages, incomes would then be forced back to the level of subsistence.

In consequence factory owners believed they had a duty to drive their workers hard. Diligently wages were kept low. Factory hours, on the other hand, were long, often stretching from before dawn until late into the night, punctuated by no more than two or three short breaks. Few industrialists showed any concern for the safety of those they employed who were exposed to danger both from the unguarded machines – one writer reported that in a walk around Manchester a person would see so many maimed operatives that it was like being "in the midst of an army just returned from a campaign" – and from the stifling atmosphere which, in the case of textile mills, was usually polluted with fibrous dust which produced serious nose, throat, and chest infections. *Factory workers*

Many of those who entered the factories had been earlier employed in their own homes. They were no strangers to hard work. But though their former life had made them familiar with long hours and poor pay, it had also given them a certain independence. Within limits they had been free to work when they wanted and at a pace they set themselves. Now things were very different. The worker had to travel to and from the factory at times laid down by his employer and while there was constantly under the surveillance of an overseer who made sure that he did not slack. The speed at which he worked was now governed by power-driven machines. Regimented, en-

(*Opposite*) Factory children scavenging for food in pigs' troughs, 1840.

snared by frustrating regulations, the newcomer soon came to hate his place of work and pined for the "good old days."

Above we read what an anonymous cotton spinner thought of his employers. Here is what he had to say about his fellow workers and the lives that they led:

The workmen in general are an inoffensive, unassuming set of well-informed men, though how they acquire their information is almost a mystery to me. They are docile and tractable, if not goaded too much; but this is not to be wondered at, when we consider that they are trained to work from six years old, from five in a morning to eight and nine at night. Let one of the advocates for obedience to his master take his stand in an avenue leading to a factory a little before five o'clock in the morning, and observe the squalid appearance of the little infants and their parents taken from their beds at so early an hour in all kinds of weather; let him examine the miserable pittance of food, chiefly composed of water gruel and oatcake broken into it, a little salt, and sometimes coloured with a little milk, together with a few potatoes, and a bit of bacon or fat for dinner. . . . The negro slave in the West Indies, if he works under a scorching sun, has probably a little breeze of air sometimes to fan him: he has a space of ground, and time allowed to cultivate it. The English spinner slave has no enjoyment of the open atmosphere and breezes of heaven. Locked up in factories eight storeys high, he has no relaxation till the ponderous engine stops, and then he goes home to get refreshed for the next day; no time for sweet association with his family; they are all alike fatigued and exhausted.

The doctrine of laissez-faire favoured the employer. It set him free to pay low wages. For the worker, however, the freedom promised by Adam Smith was of little worth; true he was at liberty to reject those wages, but if he did so he was without a job. The policy seemed very unfair. The passage of the Combination Acts (1799 and 1800) gave weight to his belief that there was one law for the rich, another for the poor. Parliament, while maintaining that it was not its business to say how manufacturers should treat their workers, did not hesitate to act in order to stop working people from combining together. Such combinations were now declared "conspiracies in restraint of trade". Although the second of the two Acts also prohibited the formation of employers' organizations, this ban had little effect.

Trade unionism was established in Britain long before 1750.

The early unions were local bodies, mainly for skilled craftsmen in the towns. Though, like later trade unions, they were formed to maintain and improve the conditions of employment of their members, they tended to be less militant than many which appeared during the latter part of the Industrial Revolution, and often confined their activities to the provision of sick and funeral benefits, in the manner of a fraternal organization or social club.

The growth of the factory system, by gathering large numbers of men together in one work place, brought new opportunities for unions to be formed. At the same time it created conditions which made such bodies necessary. Together the workers faced the rigours of factory life; they shared the suffering and frustrations and joined with one another in voicing their discontent. They soon realized that only by united action did they stand any chance of forcing an employer to make improvements. As might be expected, it was among operatives in the cotton spinning factories of Lancashire that trade unionism spread most rapidly in the years immediately preceding the Combination Acts.

*Unionism:
a new impetus*

These Acts were not repealed until 1824. Even during their period of operation, however, some unions managed to function, often evading the law by organizing as benefit societies. But in general the first quarter of the nineteenth century was a time of repression, the ruling classes being afraid that the mob would take over in Britain as it had done in France. Parliament passed a number of stern measures. Lord Byron was incensed by one of these, a Bill to raise the penalty for breaking a machine from fourteen years' exile in a penal colony to death by hanging. In 1812, making his first speech in the House of Lords, he said:

*Lord Byron
on "the mob"*

You call these men a mob . . . are we aware of our obligations to a mob? It is the mob that labour in your fields and serve in your houses, that man your Navy and recruit your Army that have enabled you to defy all the world and can defy you also when neglect and calamity have driven them to despair. . . .

I have been in some of the most oppressed provinces of Turkey but never under the most despotic of infidel governments did I behold such squalid wretchedness as I have seen since my return to the very heart of a Christian country.

But Lord Byron did not represent the views of most property owners, to whom fear continued to cling like an unrelenting burr. There was no let-up in the government's determination to stamp out social unrest, even when the war with France came to an end in 1815. The economic depression that then followed was sufficient to keep alive the threat of rebellion. Not until there were signs that agriculture, commerce, and industry were all well on the way to recovery did the government change its tough line. At last, in 1824, trade unions were free to operate again in the open.

Among unions that now came into being were some that represented the technicians of the new mechanical age – the Journeymen Steam Engine and Machine Makers' Friendly Society, the Steam Engine Makers' Society, and the United Machine Workers' Association. Like earlier associations of craftsmen, they were not militant bodies and were mostly concerned with the provision of welfare services for their members.

At the same time there was another development which, though short-lived, was certainly more dramatic. This involved large numbers of unskilled and semi-skilled workers. They were not only discontented about such matters as low wages and long hours, but were highly critical of society in general. Their aim was revolution.

The Grand National Since the repeal of the Combination Acts some unions had started to organize on a national, rather than a local, basis. During what may be called the revolutionary period of British trade unionism (1829–36), yet another dimension was added; attempts were now made to form organizations which, as well as being national, included workers from many different industries, even farming. Such a body was a *trades* union. By far the largest was the Grand National Consolidated Trades Union, which was formed in 1834. Within a few months it had well over half a million members.

The Grand National was largely the product of one man's dream. Robert Owen, factory owner and early socialist, saw it as the means to transform society. By making use of the general strike as a weapon, it was to take over the government of the whole country in the name of the working class. Employers would soon become unnecessary, production and distribution having been placed in the charge of cooperative societies.

Though it swiftly rallied widespread support, the seeds of the Grand National's failure were sown within a few weeks of its foundation. Indeed, the very speed of its growth contributed to its downfall. The union was unable to control the huge membership and branches rushed into local strikes which soon used up the very limited financial resources. The government made matters worse by encouraging employers to resist their workers' demands. Many industrialists precipitated conflicts by insisting that their employees sign a pledge to renounce any association with the Grand National. If they refused to accept this "document," as did fifteen hundred workers at Derby, they were locked out until they changed their minds. By the end of 1835 the Grand National had ceased to exist.

Employers combine

Employers were united in their hostility to trade unionism, particularly when it took such a threatening form as the Grand National. Collective action was not new to them. Though condemning their workers' right to combine, they had set up numerous associations themselves in order to fix prices and regulate conditions of sale. Cotton manufacturers were represented on the Committee for the Protection and Encouragement of Trade, established at Manchester in 1774. A few years later a similar organization came into existence for the woollen industry; this was not only vigorous in attacking trade unions, but also fought against the export of wool and textile machinery. In the metal trades the makers of cutlery, files, nails, and tools each had their own organizations. The iron-

Sheffield: an industrial town, 1850.

masters too were busy; records show that several of their associations held regular quarterly meetings and charged members an annual subscription of a guinea. By the early nineteenth century ironmasters were trying to coordinate their policies; associations communicated with each other and sometimes sent representatives to each other's meetings.

One of the most interesting of these early bodies was the General Chamber of Manufacturers of Great Britain, which was founded in 1785, largely due to the efforts of Josiah Wedgwood. It brought together employers from a number of different industries with a common interest in opposing the policies of the government. In particular, members disliked the new tax proposals and the planned commercial treaty with Ireland. By exerting pressure on Members of Parliament, the General Chamber was able to persuade the government to modify its economic programme.

A painful adjustment   During the Industrial Revolution both manufacturers and workers had to adjust to changed circumstances. The manufacturer, needing to make profits if his business was to expand, believed that he could prosper only by keeping wages low. To improve working conditions would eat into those profits. The demands of his workers were seen as a threat to his very livelihood. It was little wonder that he was fearful of trade unions.

As for the worker, he was still probably a country man at heart. While Owen dreamed of a bright new Britain, the worker looked nostalgically back to what had once been. Illiterate and ignorant, like many who joined the Grand National, he was apprehensive of the future.

It was not until after 1850, by which time the country had begun to reap the fruits of industrialization, that masters and men began to show any understanding of each other's problems and difficulties. Then, with the economy prospering, employers were at last willing to make concessions over wages and hours. Only then, as prosperity filtered down to it, did a new generation of workers start coming to terms with life in an industrial society.

CHAPTER SIX

The Price of Progress

The Industrial Revolution brought fundamental changes to the lives of many people. Whether these were for better or worse is no easy matter to decide. How, in the ledger of history, does one balance increases in production against human discontent and suffering? With hindsight we can argue that the social and economic disruption, which caused widespread distress, was the price that had to be paid for long-term improvements in standards of living. But for those who actually experienced hardship there was little comfort in the promise of better times to come.

Not everyone, of course, was dissatisfied with events. For some industrialization was an unqualified boon. The land-owning aristocracy, for example, grew even more prosperous as a result of the inflated rents which could now be charged for land required for mining, factories, railways, and urban development. In consequence, the political supremacy that they had long enjoyed stayed unchallenged until the 1830's. Their increased wealth was displayed in the huge new houses which many built and by the packs of fox hounds that they sported. *Those who gained*

Industrial capitalists also found a new affluence. Numbering many who had risen from modest, though rarely downright poor, beginnings, this group was well content with the changes that were taking place. Not that every man who entered business wound up making a fortune. Some, like Henry Cort and John Roebuck, lost heavily and went bankrupt. But such failures only made other manufacturers the more determined to pursue their interests with energy and ruthlessness. Along with merchants, bankers, and lawyers, with whom they often associated in their business activities, industrialists made up the middle class, a stratum in society which, as it became economically more powerful, began to demand political rights.

73

Until 1832 those who sat in both Houses of Parliament mostly represented Britain's landowners. The vast majority of the population was without the vote. By the Reform Act of that year, however, following intense pressure from the middle class, the franchise was enlarged. For the first time industrial centres like Manchester, Sheffield, Birmingham, Wolverhampton, and Sunderland were able to elect their own Members of Parliament. Landowning interests, weakened by the redistribution of seats, now had to share power in the Commons with representatives from the manufacturing districts.

Less fortunate

In general, therefore, both the upper and middle classes benefited from the Industrial Revolution. But what of the mass of people, the "lower orders" as they were called? Without doubt many of these found life very hard. It was, perhaps, the women and children who suffered most. Labouring alongside the men in factory and mine, they endured conditions which were often so appalling that they even shocked Parliament into doing something about them. At a time when sufficient hands were difficult to come by, industrialists were always ready to employ women and children, for they were cheap and more submissive than their male counterparts.

Women

In earlier times a woman, though she might have to labour in the fields or sit for long hours at the cottage loom, was able, nevertheless, to take some time off to attend to her duties as mother and wife. But factory life robbed her of the chance to do this. Now she was kept away from her home and family for upward of ten hours daily. If she had a young child, he was probably left, as one writer suggested, in the charge of "some little girl or aged woman, who is hired for a trifle, and whose services are equivalent to the reward".

But though the lot of the factory woman was not easy, it was very much better than that of the women who worked underground in the mines. Some laboured as "bearers", carrying the coal from where it was dug to the pit head in baskets strapped to their backs. Others, like Betty Harris, dragged their heavy loads behind them:

I have a belt round my waist, and a chain passing between my legs, and I go on my hands and feet. The road is very steep, and we have to hold by a rope; and when there is no rope, by anything we can catch hold of. There are six women and about six boys and girls in the pit I work in; it is very hard work for a woman. The pit is very

In the mines: "I have a belt round my waist, and a chain passing between my legs, and I go on my hands and feet." (Betty Harris).

wet where I work, and the water comes over our clog-tops always, and I have seen it up to my thighs; it rains in at the roof terribly. My clothes are wet through almost all day long.

Child labour

Boys and girls were not supposed to be employed until they had reached the age of six, but as there was no means of checking just how old a child might be, many started work when they were even younger. Parents, used to the idea of children working, relied upon the earnings of their youngsters to swell the family income. Made to work the same long hours as adults, children often were prevented from falling asleep on the job by the whips or straps of the overseers. In spite of this, drowsy infants sometimes fell into moving machinery, with disastrous consequences.

In 1832 a Select Committee of the House of Commons was appointed to collect evidence about the way that factory children were treated. Michael Sadler, its chairman, was an ardent Churchman; though a Leeds businessman, he did not believe, like many of his class, that profits could be maintained only by exploiting the young. Among the many witnesses who appeared before Sadler's Committee was Elizabeth Bentley:

Age 23, lives at Leeds, began work at the age of six in Mr Busk's flaxmill, as a little doffer. Hours 5 A.M. till 9 P.M. when they were "thronged", otherwise 6 A.M. to 7 at night, with 40 minutes for meal at noon.

Do you consider doffing a laborious employment? Explain what you had to do.

75

When the frames are full, they have to stop the frames, and take the flyers off, and take the full bobbins off, and carry them to the roller; and then put empty ones on, and set the frame going again.

Does that keep you constantly on your feet?

Yes, there are so many frames, and they run so quick.

Your labour is very excessive?

Yes; you have not time for anything.

Suppose you flagged a little, or were too late, what would they do?

Strap us.

Girls as well as boys?

Yes.

Have you ever been strapped?

Yes.

Severely?

Yes. . . .

In what part of the mill did you work?

In the card-room.

It was exceedingly dusty?

Yes.

Did it affect your health?

Yes; it was so dusty, the dust got upon my lungs, and the work was so hard: I was middling strong when I went there, but the work was so bad; I got so bad in health, that when I pulled the baskets down, I pulled my bones out of their places. . . .

You are considerably deformed in your person in consequence of this labour?

Yes, I am.

"*Trappers*"   There were few industries that did not make use of child labour. Some boys and girls were taken into the coal mines to work when they were only four or five, though eight was the more usual starting age. Numbers of these were employed as "trappers"; they sat in the dark with a string in their hands, which they tugged to open a "trap", or door, when they heard a coal cart approaching. J. R. Leifchild, writing in 1853, was concerned about youngsters being lost in the "passages of the dark mine". He knew of a little boy who had been missing in a Welsh pit for seventy-two hours; when found he had been in a very weak state. But trappers, he was told, were in no such danger: "The trappers are stationary, and if found away from their doors are thumped and threatened. . . . Many sit there, too, in fear of the hobgoblins to be met within the pit; and the

reputation of hobgoblins is sustained for their good behaviour."

Throughout the Industrial Revolution most of the upper *Reformers* and middle classes were indifferent to the hardships and dangers faced by workers. There were, however, a few men who tried to bring about reforms; these included Anthony Ashley (later Lord Shaftesbury), Richard Oastler, Robert Owen, and Michael Sadler. They concentrated their efforts on improving the working conditions of children. But it was no easy task to persuade Parliament to act and it was not until 1833 that they won an important victory.

In that year the first really effective Factory Act was passed, *Factory* though it dealt only with the employment of children in textile *legislation* mills. No child was to start such work until he was nine years old; children between nine and thirteen were restricted to a nine-hour working day; while the limit for those between

Market for hiring children which was held each week at Spitalfields, London, under the supervision of the police.

Children operating
a steam-driven
envelope machine.

thirteen and eighteen was set at twelve hours: all night work
was prohibited. Reformers had complained about the lack of
education in the life of a young worker. The Act laid down
that every child who was restricted to a nine-hour day should
"attend some school". The success of this legislation owed
much to the wise provision that full-time government inspectors be appointed to make sure that the law was carried out.

In 1842, despite fierce opposition from wealthy coal owners
in the House of Lords, Parliament banned the employment
underground of women, girls, and boys who were not yet ten

years of age. This measure, introduced by Ashley, also established mines inspectors.

Two more Factory Acts were passed in 1844 and 1847, though like the one in 1833, they applied only to the textile industries. As a result of these the hours of children under thirteen were limited to six and a half, while women and young persons between thirteen and eighteen achieved a ten-hour working day. In addition, the fencing of dangerous machinery was now made the manufacturer's responsibility.

By 1850, however, nothing had been done still to safeguard women and children working in industries which made such goods as paper, matches, glass, and earthenware, many of whom were exposed to health hazards far worse than those encountered by textile operatives.

So far attention has been focused on the problems faced by the industrial labourer while at work. But what of his life away from the factory or workshop? The effects of industrialization were felt here too. Workers had to be housed near where they were employed, with the result that new towns mushroomed around the coalfields of the North and Midlands. As well as adjusting to novel conditions of labour, many of these workers had to get used to the equally new experience of being town dwellers.

Town life

Between 1801 and 1851 the joint population of Manchester and Salford rose from 90,000 to 400,000. Other towns showed similar increases, e.g. Blackburn (12,000 to 65,000), Bradford (13,000 to 104,000), Leeds (53,000 to 172,000) and Sheffield (46,000 to 135,000). The very speed of this urban growth brought difficulties. There was no time for planned development. In the absence of any state control the way was clear for jerry-builders to grow rich at the cost of the unfortunates who had no choice but to live in the shoddy buildings which they erected.

These houses were set back to back in rows, which meant that unless placed at the end of a row, the occupants of a house had different neighbours across three of their walls. Overcrowding was common, and as the walls were usually only of half-brick thickness, these buildings were noisy places. Sanitary facilities were primitive, with often twenty or more families sharing the same privies and drawing water from a single pump or tap which might be turned on only for a limited

Housing

period each day. In many districts water had to be obtained from carriers who came around with their carts; in Bradford, for example, three gallons could be purchased for a penny. All windows were taxed until 1825, when the law was relaxed to allow each house to have eight windows tax-free. This meant that rooms and stairways were both poorly lit and badly ventilated.

Health   Towns were unhealthy places in which to live. Authorities did little about the rubbish which accumulated in the streets or polluted waterways, so that diseases like typhoid, typhus, smallpox, and measles took a heavy toll. In 1832 a new menace appeared – cholera. Within a few months it had claimed more than thirteen thousand victims. The cholera epidemic of 1848–49 was even worse, bringing about the deaths of eighty thousand people. It was widely believed that these diseases were caused by bad air. The fact that they were more prevalent in urban areas was explained by the greater volume of foul air to be found in towns. Considering this belief, it is understandable that people did not wish to open windows, even when they had them in their houses.

Edwin   Disease is no respecter of persons. Although the worse
Chadwick's conditions were in those areas where industrial workers lived,
Report   outbreaks of cholera, typhus, and smallpox soon spread to the wealthier parts of towns. During the 1840's, therefore, the government came under pressure to make towns healthier. It initiated a number of inquiries to find out just how bad things were and what could be done to bring about improvements. The most important of these was undertaken by Edwin Chadwick. In his *Report on the Sanitary Condition of the Labouring Population* (1842), Chadwick showed that the life expectancy of a town worker was much shorter than that of a country man. The average age of death for workers in industrial Manchester was seventeen, while for those in the rural county of Rutlandshire it was thirty-eight. He also pointed out that there was a marked difference between the number of years lived by the various social classes. In Leeds, for example, the average life of a gentleman was forty-four years, a tradesman twenty-seven years, and an industrial operative nineteen years. For similar groups in Liverpool the figures were thirty-five, twenty-two, and fifteen.

Urban life, with its problems, was part of the price which

large numbers of workers had to pay for industrialization. As Chadwick indicated, workers found themselves in a situation where they possessed neither the means nor the will to improve their lot:

The workmen's "location", as it is termed, is generally governed by his work, near which he must reside . . . if he wishes to have a house, he must avail himself of the first vacancy that presents itself; if there happen to be more houses vacant than one, the houses usually being of the same class, little range of choice is thereby presented to him. . . .

The individual labourer has little or no power over the internal structure and economy of the dwelling which has fallen to his lot. If the water be not laid on in the other houses in the street, or if it be unprovided with proper receptacles for refuse, it is not in the power of any individual workman who may perceive the advantage of such accommodations to procure them. He has as little control over the external economy of his residence as of the structure of the street before it, whether it shall be paved or unpaved, drained or undrained. . . . [Before long] he appears to be insensible to anything but changes of temperature.

F

CHAPTER SEVEN

Industrialization in the United States

When the American War of Independence came to an end in
1783 the population of the United States numbered about
three millions, most of whom lived in a broad belt of land
which ran along the eastern coast for over a thousand miles.
There were no really large cities; Philadelphia, the biggest,
had fewer than 40,000 inhabitants. To the west, across the
Allegheny Mountains, the American Indian still reigned
supreme.

*Westward
expansion*
Between 1783 and 1850, while Britain was in the throes of
the Industrial Revolution, Americans were involved in a different kind of upheaval. The young nation was on the move
westward. "Old America seems to be breaking up", one obser-
ver commented in 1817. Travelling along the major turnpike
which led to Ohio, he noted: "We are seldom out of sight of
family groups behind and before us." The developments
described in this chapter must be seen against the background
of this migration.

*Manufacturers'
problems*
Industrialization in America, which had its beginnings
during this same period, proceeded at a slower pace than in
Britain. Indeed, it was not until after the Civil War that its
full effects were felt. One major reason for this was the existence of an apparently limitless supply of unsettled land. It
made problems for America's manufacturers. Many early
industrialists, for example, found it difficult to raise capital as
their most likely source, the merchants, preferred to use their
money to speculate in land. But even when they had sufficient
funds, there was the further problem of obtaining and keeping
a trained labour force. Skilled workers, many of whom had but
recently arrived from Europe, were just the sort of adventurous people to be attracted by opportunities in the west.
Some plants had to shut down because they could not retain
82 sufficient labour. A glassworks in Pennsylvania was among

The *Mississippi*, a locomotive built in England for use in the United States, 1834.

these; although the owner, Baron Stiegel, imported workmen from Europe, he was unable to hold them once they had worked off the cost of their passage.

American manufacturers were less willing to make use of steam power than their counterparts in Britain. This was understandable in a country where, with an abundance of rivers and streams, waterwheels were both cheap and simple to run. Nevertheless, industrial progress suffered as a result. Production was lost because waterwheels became inactive in times of drought or freezing. Even in Britain this had proved a drawback; in parts of America, where the extremes of temperature were often much greater, it could mean that a mill or workshop was unable to function for many weeks of each year. The large government armoury at Springfield, Massachusetts, which depended for power on a small tributary of the Connecticut River, was regularly affected during the months of December, January, February, and July.

Although the construction of turnpikes was well under way by the early nineteenth century, vast areas of the country were served only by tracks which were rutted hard by the sun and

Dependence on water

83

turned into morasses by the rain. In winter new roads and old tracks alike might be closed by heavy falls of snow. Many manufacturers relied upon river craft to supply them with raw materials or for the dispatch of their goods, but here too the weather limited operations, often confining shipments to spring, summer, and autumn. The lack of adequate transportation was another factor retarding industrial development.

Britain guards
her secrets
Apart from these internal problems, America's manufacturers had to contend with measures passed by the British Parliament to safeguard that country's industrial lead. During the second half of the eighteenth century Parliament had forbade the export of textile machines, as well as plans or models of them. A similar prohibition applied to tools used in the iron industry. There was even an attempt to prevent trained operatives from emigrating, and anyone caught persuading them to do so was severely punished. For a time at least, such restrictions proved frustrating to American manufacturers and made them dependent for new machinery on smuggled information or inventions produced at home.

1783–1815
The first phase of industrialization in the United States took place between 1783 and 1815. Proud of having achieved political independence, it was not long before the young country looked to extend this newly won freedom to the economic sphere as well. The need to do so was heightened by the war between Britain and France which broke out in 1793 and soon involved most of the leading states in western Europe. At first, neutral Americans profited from the sale of agricultural products to the belligerents, an expansion in trade which also led to a boom in shipbuilding; the tonnage of American merchant shipping rose from 202,000 in 1789 to 1,425,000 in 1810. In exchange America imported a wide range of manufactured goods from Europe, in particular from Britain. These included glass, cutlery, pottery, edged tools, blankets, woollen cloth, linen, and cotton prints. After 1807, however, this trade was seriously interrupted. There were a number of reasons for this: first, American shipping began to be hindered by both the British and the French; second, Congress retaliated by passing an Embargo Act which stopped the country's ships from sailing to foreign ports; and third, between 1812 and 1814 the United States was at war with Britain. In consequence, domestic producers were stimulated to supply some

84

at least of the manufactured goods that could no longer be obtained from abroad.

But this impulse was short lived. Once the war was at an end there was a renewed influx of goods from Britain's manufacturers, many of whom were prepared to sell at low prices and wait long periods for payment in an effort to strangle at birth America's young industries. Henry Brougham, speaking in the House of Commons, even suggested that it was "well worth while to incur a loss upon the first exportation, in order, by the glut, to stifle in the cradle these rising manufactures in the United States, which the war has forced into existence, contrary to the natural order of things". Faced with such a challenge, American manufacturers demanded protection, and in 1817 a general tariff Act was passed which imposed duties on imported cotton, woollen, and linen cloth, boots and shoes, hats, glassware, earthenware, writing paper, and many other products. Continuance of this protective policy was not universally welcomed, merchants and farmers being among those who disliked it.

The second phase of industrialization ran from 1815 to about 1840. It was a period of steady progress. Many small factories sprang up, but shortages of capital and labour restricted the size of most enterprises. At the same time, manufacturers still mainly relied on waterwheels to power their machinery, and on waterways for the distribution of their goods.

It was not until the third phase, 1840 to 1860, that manufacturing developed at a rapid pace. The introduction of steam power led to a growth in the size of many factories. The iron industry was revolutionized by the substitution of coal for wood in the smelting process. The problem of transportation was largely solved by the rise of the railways. Although agriculture remained the chief concern of most Americans, by 1860 there were few who had not felt some effects of the Industrial Revolution now beginning to transform the country.

In spite of the precautions British manufacturers took to safeguard their machinery, knowledge of new industrial processes soon found its way across the Atlantic. The cotton industry was among the first to be affected and within a few years of the invention of the spinning jenny, a similar machine

Samuel Slater's factory, established at Pawtucket, Rhode Island, 1790.

was in operation in Philadelphia. In 1786 Robert and Alexander Barr, who had emigrated from Scotland to Massachusetts, built carding and spinning machines which closely resembled the models patented by Arkwright in England. The following year a cotton factory was set up at Beverly, Massachusetts, but it ran into difficulties, as did a number of small mills subsequently opened. A major problem was to find a means of powering the new machinery; for a time horses were used before giving way to waterwheels.

Samuel Slater   The first successful factory was established at Pawtucket, Rhode Island, in 1790 by Samuel Slater, a skilled mechanic who had worked for several years in one of Arkwright's mills in England. Slater had travelled to America armed with details of the water frame that he had painstakingly memorized. He entered into partnership with William Almy and Moses Brown, both wealthy men, his role being to construct machinery and supervise the erection of a factory. Although a handicraft cotton industry already flourished in the district, it was still necessary to train operatives for the new machines, so Slater set up a school for this purpose. Andrew Jackson, U. S. President during the 1830's, called Slater the "father of American manufactures".

Shortly after the firm of Almy, Brown and Slater opened its Pawtucket factory, Eli Whitney patented his cotton gin, thereby ensuring a plentiful supply of raw material. This, coupled with the obvious success of the enterprise, prompted others to follow Slater's example and by the end of the century similar mills were in operation in various parts of New England.

As in Britain, at first the factory system was confined to the carding and spinning of cloth. It was not until 1814 that the power loom was brought into use by Francis C. Lowell. The factory which he established at Waltham, Massachusetts, was different from any previously known, for he introduced both spinning and weaving machines under the same roof. *Francis C. Lowell*

But despite these early advances, factory production developed slowly, even in the cotton industry. Not till the 1840's, when capital was more readily available to manufacturers, did mechanization and the spread of factories make significant headway. Progress at this time was also helped by the passage of a new patents law in 1836, leading to a spectacular increase in inventions. Whereas before that date an average of twenty-five patents a year had been taken out, the number subsequently rose to several hundred annually. In addition, the use of steam engines became more widespread, thereby liberating manufacturers from the seasonal limitations of water power, as well as enabling them to erect mills or workshops where no rivers existed.

Steam had been used to power machinery in the United States from as early as 1800. Foremost among the pioneers to experiment with its application was Oliver Evans. In 1804 this remarkable engineer drove a wagon propelled by steam through the streets of Philadelphia. About the same time he opened a works in that city for the production of engines, and followed it a few years later with another plant in Pittsburgh. Evans concentrated his attentions on developing steam power to drive ships. The engines manufactured by Boulton and Watt in England were large, complex, costly to build and maintain, and generally unsuitable for transportation pur- *Steam power* poses. Evans succeeded in perfecting a steam engine which, though simple and cheap, generated considerable power. It went into production and was soon in use in large numbers of sea and river craft. The propulsion of ships was to be steam's major role for many years to come. Even as late as 1838 industry accounted for only a small fraction of the nation's total steam power, three fifths of which was employed in shipping.

Iron   Industrialization in America, as in Britain, was closely associated with an increased use of iron. Early in the nineteenth century it was produced in most states, in numerous little smelting mills. Despite the smallness of these undertakings, the capital required was often more than a single ironmaster could find and he became dependent upon money invested by merchants, wealthy farmers, professional men, and others. Ironmasters relied on local supplies of ore and fuel, and usually sold their output to people living within the neighbouring district. Production was mainly of iron bars and plates, drawn to different shapes and sizes, which could be worked up by blacksmith or farmer into horseshoes, wagon tyres, chains, nails, tools, and many other articles. In addition, ironmasters made some household goods, including pots, pans, and kettles. Specialization in the manufacture of iron products made little progress until the 1820's, and even then, iron factories tended to stay close to smelting works.

Technical change occurred in the American iron industry in a different order from that which had transformed its counterpart in Britain. In the United States the processes of rolling and puddling were well established before there was any large-scale substitution of coal for wood at the smelting stage. The reason for the reversal in order is not hard to understand: in Britain the impulse for change had been a shortage of charcoal, while in America, where there was an abundance of timber, it was a scarcity of labour which first led to innovation. The introduction of coal into the blast furnaces, though delayed, was an important development, however, for it made possible the use of much larger furnaces, which in turn led to greatly increased yields.

By 1860 the iron industry had been revolutionized. Though it was still primarily concerned with the needs of a basically agricultural society, there were growing demands for metal ships, for factory machinery and, from the new railways, for locomotives, rolling stock, and rails. The industry was becoming centralized in a number of towns, where blast furnaces were sited alongside rolling mills. The largest of these was Pittsburgh; others included Philadelphia, Scranton, Cincinnati, Baltimore, and St. Louis.

The growth of such towns gave a boost to coal production. *Coal* Although mining took place in several states, the two main coal areas were both in Pennsylvania, where rich deposits of anthracite were available in the northeast, while bituminous coal was located in the Pittsburgh-Connellsville district. So long as wood remained the major fuel for domestic and industrial purposes only limited demands were made on these resources, but the situation began to change about 1840. Developments in the iron industry and in transportation led to an increased output of coal, especially of anthracite.

Throughout much of the period up to the Civil War, coal was mainly transported by water, though from the 1840's onward, railways started to take over some of this traffic. The movement of anthracite had been facilitated during the 1820's by the construction of canals, such as the Delaware and Hudson, the Morris, and the Lehigh. Mines and canals were often jointly owned by companies that had control over large amounts of capital. In the bituminous districts, however, there were plenty of natural waterways; this, coupled with the fact that the coal was near the surface and easy to mine, meant that production could be carried out by small operators.

Whereas in Britain the siting of manufacturing plants soon *Locations* became dependent upon their proximity to supplies of coal, in *for industry* America access to water power and water transportation facilities were more important factors in determining where industry was located. The earliest works were established on the coast or along the numerous rivers that fed into the Atlantic. Shipbuilding was a leading industry in colonial times, not only supplying Britain with ships, but with masts, spars, and naval stores as well. Even when the westward movement got under way and overland routes were opened up, new towns still tended to grow up at key points on rivers. Among these were Pittsburgh, Cincinnati, St. Louis, and Louisville, all of which became centres of factory production. Where natural waterways were inadequate, canals were constructed, especi-

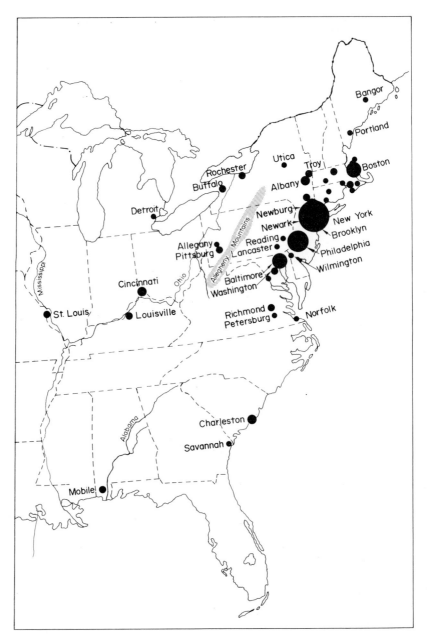

Map showing the main centres of population in the United States, *c.* 1845.

ally during the 1820's when a canal fever gripped the country similar to that which had occurred in Britain some forty years earlier. This brought new manufacturing cities like Rochester, New York, into existence and added to the industrial activities of others, such as New York, Buffalo, and Philadelphia.

Shipbuilding has already been mentioned as an industry *Agricultural* which had its roots deep in colonial times. The grinding of *products* flour and the cutting of timber were also important activities in the years before independence, being among the first manufacturing processes to move outside the home into mills powered by water. After 1783 the introduction of more complex machinery led to the setting up of larger flour mills, with some localization of the industry; Baltimore, Maryland, and Richmond, Virginia, for example, became leading milling towns. But farther west, where each new frontier community usually had its own flour mill, such enterprises remained small. Manufacture also played an important part in preparing other agricultural products for market and during the first half of the nineteenth century progress was made in the processing of leather and tobacco, in brewing, in the canning of fruit and fish, and in meat packing.

Industrialization in the United States was accompanied by *The growth* rapid urbanization. In 1780 there had been only five towns *of towns* with a population of over 8,000; by 1860 there were 141 such towns, including New York with more than a million inhabitants and Philadelphia with about half that number. Many of those who swelled the urban population were immigrants. Up to 1825 fewer than 10,000 immigrants a year had arrived in the United States, but after that date a sharp rise began. In 1840 the figure reached 100,000 and by 1854 was over 400,000. Events in Europe, for example the potato famine in Ireland and the Crimean War, caused fluctuations in numbers, but by 1860 it was estimated that there were four million foreign-born settlers in the country.

As in Britain, the working classes in the new towns encountered many problems; jerry-built housing, overcrowded conditions, poor sanitation, disease, few schools, and a lack of recreational facilities. Here is a description of part of New York City in 1853:

In Oliver Street, Fourth Ward, is a miserable rear dwelling, 6 feet by 30, two storeys and garret, three rooms on each of the first and second floors, and four in the attic – in all, ten small apartments, which contain 14 families. The entrance is through a narrow, dirty alley, and the yard and appendages of the filthiest kind. . . . In Cherry Street, a "tenement house", on two lots, extending back from the street 150 feet, five storeys above the basement, so arranged as to contain 120 families, or more than 500 persons. A small room and bedroom are allowed each family in this building, which is of the better class; but the direful consequence of imperfect ventilation and overcrowding are severely felt.

Blame the So long as there was a shortage of labour, working conditions
immigrants! in America were generally better than in Britain. But it was the skilled workers that profited most from this scarcity. The unskilled, even before the flood of immigrants removed any advantage they might have from labour being in short supply, often worked as long as fourteen hours a day for wages that were barely adequate to support existence. Once the number of immigrants began to mount, the unskilled were swift to charge the newcomers with depressing wages. In 1840, one newspaper reported:

Our labouring men, native and naturalized, are met at every turn and every avenue of employment, with recently imported workmen from the low wage countries of the old world. Our public improvements, railroads and canals are thronged with foreigners. They fill our large cities, reduce the wages of labour, and increase the hardships of the old settler.

Child labour Many textile manufacturers, particularly in New England, relied heavily on the use of child labour in their mills. Some, modelling their factories on the one established by Lowell at Waltham, attended to the welfare of the boys and girls they employed. Others were less considerate and, like many a British industrialist, treated the youngsters as though they had no more feelings than the machines around them. A report printed in the *Mechanics' Free Press* in 1830 spoke of factory children who were "as ignorant as Arabs of the Desert", fewer than one sixth of them being capable of reading or writing their own name. Massachusetts passed a law in 1837 requiring that all employees who were under fifteen years of age receive three months' schooling a year, but as
92 another thirty years were to go by before any system of inspec-

tion was established, the measure had a very limited effect. New Hampshire was probably the first state to legislate about children's hours, restricting these to ten a day in 1847.

Trade unionism in the United States had its beginnings in the last quarter of the eighteenth century among the craftsmen in such trades as printing and shoemaking. These unions were local bodies which, in most cases, rarely had a life longer than a few years. As with similar early organizations in Britain, they combined a concern for better working conditions with an interest in sick and funeral benefits. Militancy did not play a big part in their activities, though some strikes were called as, for example, by Philadelphia's printers in 1786. The courts usually supported employers in any struggle with the unions, maintaining that workers' combinations were conspiracies against the state. *Trade unionism*

A second stage of development began in the late 1820's, from when many would date the start of modern unionism in America. Instead of operating in isolation, local unions from the same city now showed a willingness to work together in order to improve conditions. In 1827, when the carpenters of Philadelphia struck for a ten-hour day, they were at once joined by the bricklayers, glaziers, and printers. This co-operation led to the formation of a Mechanics' Union of Trade Associations, a model which was soon copied by unions in many other leading cities. During the 1830's a few unions, including the carpenters and printers, attempted to set up national organizations, but not for at least another twenty years did this movement make any significant headway.

By comparison with later achievements, trade unions gained little in the period before the Civil War. Their greatest success was in obtaining shorter hours for members: by the 1850's the principle of a ten-hour working day had been accepted by numerous employers and some states had even passed laws to enforce it. Apart from demanding better labour conditions, the unions also campaigned for other reforms; these included free schools, equal taxation, abolition of imprisonment for debt, and the direct election of public officials. By so doing they helped to focus attention on a number of issues which could not be ignored much longer.

The census of 1860 disclosed that over a sixth of the population of the United States was employed in, or was directly dependent upon, manufacturing enterprises; large numbers more were engaged in the production of raw materials for industry or in the distribution of its goods. Within less than fifty years the country had moved from a position of economic dependence on Europe to one in which it was able to satisfy nearly all of its own industrial requirements. Thanks to the millions of immigrants that had come to its shores there was no longer a shortage of labour. These same immigrants had helped to solve the transportation problem, it being largely due to their efforts that the nation already had thirty thousand miles of railways. There was now sufficient capital to meet the growing needs of industrial development. The bulk of this wealth, however, lay in the northern states. Resentful at being economically dominated by these states, the South demanded separatism, a cause for which it was prepared to fight. Not until this conflict was resolved by the Civil War could the United States fully exploit its enormous industrial potential. Only then would this vast country feel the whole impact of its Industrial Revolution.

CHAPTER EIGHT

The Golden Years

The term Industrial Revolution was probably first used by the French economist Blanqui, early in the nineteenth century, to suggest that the economic changes taking place in Britain were as revolutionary as the political changes which had just been experienced by his own country. Later historians, as was seen in the opening chapter, tried to set this revolution within exact dates. Though such precision is no longer considered possible, we still use the term as a convenient means of identifying the first stage of industrialization, a process which through subsequent stages has continued to the present day.

This initial stage was closely associated with developments in the textile trades, the second with the capital goods industries producing machinery, engineering tools, locomotives, rolling stock, rails, and ships. As might be expected, there was no clear demarcation between the two. Although the transition began as early as the 1830's, cotton and woollen manufactures still accounted for more than half of Britain's total exports some thirty years later. *A period of transition*

Why did industrialization take a new direction in the mid-nineteenth century? One reason was the mounting overseas demand for capital goods. Other countries, including many in Europe, as yet unable to cater for their own manufacturing needs, were anxious to purchase machinery, equipment, and the means of transportation so as to become industrialized themselves. Coupled with the increased sales of textiles to Asia and Africa, this led to an unprecedented growth in Britain's exports; between 1845 and 1855 they rose at a rate of more than seven percent a year. By about 1850 Britain was firmly established as the "workshop of the world," a position it was to retain for the next quarter of a century.

It will be recalled that early in the Industrial Revolution Britain had been opposed to the selling of machinery abroad. 95

Free trade Further protection was given to the young industries by placing many restrictions on both the export and import of raw materials and goods. By the middle of the nineteenth century, however, this had changed; the nation was committed to a policy of free trade. The person who did most to bring this about was Sir Robert Peel, Prime Minister from 1841 to 1846. His government introduced a comprehensive reform of Britain's tariff system; in 1842 import duties were drastically reduced on raw materials and manufactured goods, and all duties on exports were abolished, except for coal, clay, and raw wool. Peel rightly believed that, in the long term, this policy would encourage trade and industrial development, though for a time there was certain to be a loss of revenue. To offset this, he boldly reintroduced income tax. His courage was again displayed in 1846 when, against the wishes of many in his own party, he attacked the Corn Laws. These were a long established means of giving protection to farmers, by prohibiting the importation of wheat and other grains, until home prices had reached certain fixed limits. A majority of the Members of Parliament gave him support and the legislation was repealed. There was little doubt that Peel reflected the mood of the times; the nation was no longer in need of such protective measures. Indeed, without free trade Britain

An ornate railway carriage specially built in England for the Viceroy of Egypt, 1858.

96

would not have been able to take full advantage of her growing industrial strength.

During the 1840's there was a glut of capital. People with surplus money were eager to find new, profitable forms of investment. Many turned to the railways. By 1850 more than six thousand miles of track had been laid and the basic railway network was virtually in existence. But this did not deter investors. During the next twenty years a further nine thousand miles were opened, much of which proved costly to operate. *An abundance of capital*

Railway companies were popular with investors because they offered them limited liability. Other business enterprises were less attractive because, as the law stood, investors would be made responsible for the debts of the company if it ran into financial difficulties. This meant that a person might lose not only the money that he had invested, but more besides. Limited liability, on the other hand, safeguarded the rest of his property by limiting any loss to the amount invested. Naturally there was agitation that all companies should be brought in line with the railways. After 1856, when Parliament at last responded to this pressure, it was possible for industry and commerce to tap new sources of capital, the savings of a vast army of small investors. *Limited liability*

The construction of the railways had marked effects on the production of coal and iron. The annual output of coal, which stood at 50 million tons in 1850, had more than doubled by 1870; pig iron, during the same period, rose from $2\frac{1}{4}$ million tons to about 6 million. Both industries, therefore, needed large amounts of capital. A further outlet for investors was provided by shipbuilding, an industry which was booming as a result of the expansion in trade. *Other outlets*

There was wide scope for investment at home. Nevertheless, capital was so plentiful that many Britons found it necessary to turn to overseas markets and between 1850 and 1870 there was a sharp increase in the export of money. By the latter date about £700 million pounds had been invested in foreign countries, more than a quarter of it in the United States.

The Great Exhibition, which was opened in London's Hyde Park on May 1, 1851, has been called "one of the most outstanding success stories of the nineteenth century." Certainly no single event more graphically demonstrated the economic *The Great Exhibition*

BRADSHAW'S MAP OF GREAT BRITAIN

Shewing the
RAILWAYS COMPLETED & IN PROGRESS
WITH THE
ELECTRIC TELEGRAPH LAID DOWN
& THE LINE OF NAVIGATION FROM THE PRINCIPAL SEAPORTS

1851

SCALE OF MILES

The Figures thus 12 apply to the following Lines the names of which for want of space could not be inserted on the body of the Map.

1 Sheffield Rotherham Barnsley & Wakefield Railway
2 South Stafford do
3 Shropshire Union do
4 South Yorkshire Doncaster & Goole do
5 St Helens do
6 West London do
7 Blackwall do
8 Windsor Staines & South Western do
9 Witham & Coltons do
10 Berkshire Valley do
11 Leeds Dewsbury & Manchester do
12 Dundee & Arbroath do
13 Nottingham & Mansfield do
14 Manchester & Southport do
15 Liverpool & Bury do
16 Oldham Alliance do
17 Manchester & Altrincham do
18 Rutlandshire Lancashire & Cheshire Junc do
19 Maryland Junction do
20 Cockermouth & Workington do
21 Uredston & Kendal do
22 Exeter & Exmouth do
23 Buxton & Hacken do
24 Ashburton Newton & South Devon do
25 Furness do
26 East & West Yorkshire do
27 Fleetwood Preston & West Riding Junc do
28 Gloucester & Dean Forest do
29 Monmouth & Hereford do
30 Herks & Hants do
31 Colchester Stour Valley Sudbury & Halstead do
32 Glasgow Barrhead & Kilmarnock do
33 Glasgow Paisley & Greenock do
34 Kingstown & Dublin do
35 Dublin Dundrum & Rathfarnham do
36 Rugby Leamington & Warwick do
37 Rugby & Oxford Junc do
38 Coventry & Nuneaton do
39 Warhlade do
40 Eden Blackburn Clitheroe & Ith East do

EXPLANATION

Principal Stations Marked thus ———
Intermediate do do ———
Railways in operation shown thus ———
Do in progress or for which dots have been obtained ———

Figures placed after the names of Principal Towns shew the Distance from London thus ———
The Steam Boat Track from all the Principal Ports shewing the general course of the Voyage and the Distance in Miles
The carriage roads of railway is favourably weather visible
Lines on which the Electric Telegraph is in operation

IRISH SEA

ST GEORGE'S CHANNEL

CARDIGAN BAY

BRISTOL CHANNEL

progress which Britain had made during its Industrial Revolution. Not that the remarkable show was confined to the achievements of Britain alone; it was a "Great Exhibition of the Works and Industries of all Nations", where the British public could see the latest inventions and the best designs from every part of the world.

Queen Victoria was deeply interested in the project, for her husband Albert had played an important part in planning it. Upon returning from the opening, she recorded in her diary: "This day is one of the greatest and most glorious days of our lives, with which to my pride and joy, the name of my dearly beloved Albert is for ever associated." Next day *The Times* commented:

There was yesterday witnessed a sight the like of which has never happened before, and which, in the nature of things, can never be repeated. They who were so fortunate as to see it hardly knew what most to admire, or in what form to clothe the sense of wonder, and even of majesty, which struggled within them. The edifice, the treasures of nature and art collected therein, the assemblage, and the solemnity of the occasion, all conspired to suggest something even more than sense could scan or imagination attain.

The exhibition was housed in a huge glass and iron building specially designed for the occasion by Joseph Paxton. The magazine *Punch* christened it the Crystal Palace; others called it more simply the Glass Hive. It was an enormous structure covering nineteen acres. Nearly 300,000 panes of glass were used in its construction; the iron used amounted to 4,500 tons, and there were twenty-four miles of guttering. The main building was 1,848 feet long and 408 feet wide. Some impression of its size can be gathered from the fact that three large elm trees were left to grow inside it, an arched transept being erected to cover them.

There were more than 100,000 exhibits, among which were *The exhibits* such oddities as hats made from the leaf of the cabbage tree (illustrating "the industry and discipline of the prisoners in Australian jails"), a dressing table that could be converted into a fire escape, an alarm bedstead with folding legs (at the desired time this deposited the sleeper "on his feet in the middle of the room"), and a tableau of stuffed frogs. But these

(*Opposite*) Bradshaw's railway map of Great Britain, 1851.

99

Chain forging, 1852. An important market for heavy iron chains was the expanding shipbuilding industry.

eccentricities were but a small part of the contents; in the main the exhibition was concerned with serious aspects of social and economic life, with new machinery and manufactures to the fore.

Britain's exhibits were in the western half of the building, where much space was given to the use of steam power. About sixty different engines were on display, operating such machines as pumps, hammers, cranes, and printing presses. One favourite with the crowds was a steam-driven machine that folded and gummed nearly three thousand envelopes an hour. There was also plenty of evidence of the way that steam had revolutionized transportation, both at sea and on land; large ships' engines were on view, as well as an express locomotive.

Of the United States' section a contemporary wrote:

There were two causes which gave to the productions of American industry displayed in the Great Exhibition a character totally

A Sheffield cutler at work on a knife, 1813.

distinct from that which is found in those of many other countries. In the first place whole districts are solely devoted to the pursuit of agriculture, disregarding mining, trades and manufactures; and secondly, in the United States, it is rare to find wealth so accumulated as to favour the expenditure of large sums upon articles of luxury.

More than six million visitors flocked to the Crystal Palace on the 141 days that the exhibition remained opened. That summer the nation was in the grip of "exhibition fever". The railway companies competed with each other to bring people to London, cutting fares and arranging cheap excursions. Workers formed clubs to which they made small weekly payments until they had saved up their fares. Employers even granted special holidays so that their men might take their families to Hyde Park. Henry Mayhew, writing at the time, said that for large numbers of visitors the exhibition was "more of a school than a show." Certainly to many it taught the lesson that Britain now led the world in trade and industry.

An urban population The census of 1851 showed that, for the first time, Britain's population, which had almost doubled in fifty years, was evenly distributed between town and countryside. By 1871 a majority of people lived in urban surroundings. The number employed in agriculture fell from 1,904,687 in 1851 to 1,423,854 in 1871. Industrial employment, on the other hand, rose steadily during the same period; in coal mining, from 193,111 to 315,398; in cotton manufacture, from 414,998 to 508,715; in machine making and shipbuilding, from 80,528 to 172,948; and in iron and steel, from 95,350 to 191,291.

Steel Steel production had been of minor importance during the Industrial Revolution, though a method of making steel had long been known. However, the process was costly and the steel manufacturers of Sheffield and Birmingham had concentrated their efforts on producing small articles such as cutlery. The problem, as it had been when changing pig iron to wrought iron, was one of removing impurities. The need to overcome this and find a cheaper process became pressing in the mid-century, the builders of ships and railways being eager to make use of the tougher metal. An important advance was made in 1856 when Henry Bessemer discovered that he could get rid of some impurities, carbon and silicon, by forcing air through molten iron. But the removal of phosphorus presented greater difficulty and it was not until 1878 that Sidney Gilchrist Thomas found a way of doing this. Nevertheless, steel output rose from a mere 40,000 tons in 1851 to six times that quantity twenty years later; during this time, however, manufacturers were forced to use nonphosphoric ore imported from Spain and Sweden. The "Bessemer process" was independently discovered by William Kelly in America where, because of the existence of nonphosphoric ore in the Lake Superior region, it was widely used for over fifty years.

A Golden Age In 1851 *The Economist* declared that Britain had entered a Golden Age. Already, it said, "the progress of scientific discovery has been magnificent, and its application to the arts of life more remarkable still." The next quarter of a century seemed to confirm the journal's optimism. Though it was the middle classes engaged in commerce, industry, and agriculture that benefited most from the national prosperity, there was little doubt that the "golden years" brought some

102

The Castle Grinding Mill, *c.* 1860. The steel industry in Sheffield, of which this imposing building was a part, specialized in the manufacture of cutlery.

improvement to the lives of most people.

Well over three quarters of the population still belonged to the manual labour class: for them the gains were probably less than many contemporaries suggested. Their hours and conditions of work, for example, were dependent on the bargains which they, or their trade unions, could make with employers. Not until 1867 did the government act to give male workers protection. In that year Parliament passed two Bills covering factories and workshops: a factory was defined as any building in which more than fifty persons were employed in a manufacturing process, while a workshop was a building with fewer than fifty workers. These laws provided for inspection, the setting of a maximum number of working hours a day, and a minimum starting age. But they were complicated and con-

tained many loopholes. Another eleven years were to go by
before they were revised and made effective.

Self-help   Even then, they did nothing to assist workers who were
injured while on the job. Nor did they help the man who found
himself unemployed; the only state provision for him was the
Poor Law and the workhouse. Many labourers, therefore, took
steps to protect themselves from such calamities by joining a
benefit society. Others paid small weekly premiums to one of
the many insurance companies that sprang up during the
1850's; the policies which they took out often went no farther
than to ensure them a "proper funeral" when they died. The
fact that they could afford to make even these limited provisions, however, does suggest that they were better off than in
earlier times.

During the 1850's and 1860's industrial relationships were
less troubled than they had been before. Unlike their fathers,
the present workers had been born into an industrial age;
instead of wishing to overthrow the capitalist system, they
were prepared to come to terms with it. Many more skilled
and semi-skilled jobs were now available, giving opportunities
for promotion to those who would work hard and cooperate
with their employers. The latter, for their part, enjoying the
current economic boom, were willing to grant some concessions over wages, hours, and conditions.

New unions   The golden years brought a new type of trade union into
being, a national association of skilled men who worked at the
same craft. Typical of such bodies was the Amalgamated
Society of Engineers. Unlike the unions of the 1830's, these

The fitting shop of
a locomotive works
at Newcastle-on-Tyne
in 1864.

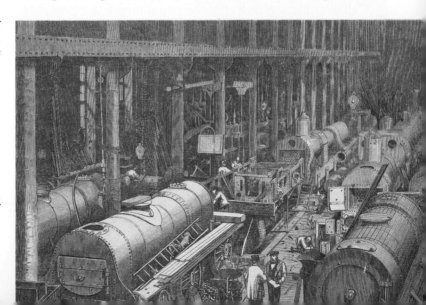

"new model" associations were reluctant to take strike action. By charging high membership dues they accumulated large funds, but these were mostly used to confer a wide range of sickness, accident, and other benefits on their members. Another innovation was their employment of paid officials, who soon became experts in union administration and organization. These full-time secretaries often met together to thrash out common policies and it was mainly due to their efforts that trade unionism was officially accepted in the early 1870's.

This final chapter has dealt with Britain at the start of a new *Conclusion* stage in its industrial development. After a long passage through turbulent waters we have seen the economy sail into calmer seas. But the prosperity which resulted from the country's dominance of trade and industry was itself not to last. By the late 1880's a decline in the rate of production was apparent, even in those branches of industry where formerly it had enjoyed superiority. It was now the turn of the United States and Germany to lead the way. Within a few years each had passed Britain in the output of steel, a vital commodity.

However the rocks which Britain was to encounter in the latter years of the century lie off our chart, as also do the currents which were to favour her industrial rivals. Let us take our leave of her and the Industrial Revolution with a passage from *The Economist*. The year is 1851; the mood one of new-found confidence. The writer, having surveyed the achievements of the past, looks forward with optimism to the future:

When we refer to a few only of the extraordinary improvements of the half-century just elapsed . . . we become convinced that it is more full of wonders than any other on record.

Of that wonderful half-century the Great Exhibition is both a fitting close and a fitting commencement of the new half century, which will, no doubt, surpass its predecessor as much as that surpassed all that went before it. . . . All who have read, and can think, must now have full confidence that the "endless progression," ever increasing in rapidity, of which the poet sang, is the destined lot of the human race.

Table of Events

1708   Thomas Newcomen invents steam pump
1709   Darby ironworks opened at Coalbrookdale
1715   Silk mill established by Thomas Lombe
1733   John Kay patents his flying shuttle
1738   John Wyatt and Lewis Paul invent a spinning machine using rollers
1748   Lewis Paul patents a carding machine
1760   Carron ironworks founded in Scotland by John Roebuck
1763   End of the Seven Years War between Britain and France
1764   Sugar Act
1765   Stamp Act. Legislation to help pay the cost of maintaining British troops in the colonies
1766   Cranage brothers develop reverberatory furnace at Coalbrookdale
1767   James Hargreaves invents spinning jenny
Iron rails cast at Coalbrookdale by Richard Reynolds
Bridgewater Canal from Manchester to Liverpool opened (The first section, from Worsley mines to Manchester, was in operation from 1761)
1769   Richard Arkwright patents water frame
James Watt patents steam engine and builds Beelzebub
1774   James Watt joins forces with Matthew Boulton
1776   The United States of America declares its independence
Adam Smith publishes *The Wealth of Nations*
1779   Samuel Crompton invents spinning mule
John Wilkinson builds an iron bridge across Severn river
1781   James Watt invents rotary engine
1784   Henry Cort and Peter Onions independently discover puddling process
1785   Edmund Cartwright designs power loom

	Parliament revokes Arkwright's patents
	General Chamber of Manufacturers of Great Britain founded
1790	Textile factory opened by Samuel Slater at Pawtucket, Rhode Island
1792	First turnpike company formed in the United States
1793	Eli Whitney invents a cotton gin
1798	Thomas Malthus publishes his first *Essay upon Population*
1799–1800	Combination Acts
1803	Territory of Louisiana purchased from France
1804	Oliver Evans develops steam power to drive ships
1807	*Clermont* steams from New York to Albany
1808	United States' Embargo Act
	John Wilkinson dies; buried in an iron coffin
1811	Cumberland Road, known as the National Pike, started at Cumberland, Maryland
1811–12	Luddite Riots; machine breaking
1812	War between Britain and the United States begins
1814	George Stephenson builds *Blucher*
	Francis C. Lowell has both spinning and weaving machinery in his Massachusetts factory
1815	Sir Humphry Davy invents a miner's safety lamp
	About this time cotton replaces tobacco as the leading export of the United States
1819	Florida purchased from Spain
	There are eleven slave and eleven free states in the United States
1824	Repeal of Combination Acts
1825	Stockton and Darlington railway opened
	Western section of the Erie Canal opened
1829	*Stourbridge Lion*, an English-built locomotive, has trial run in the United States
	Stephenson's *Rocket* wins Rainhill Trials
1830	Liverpool and Manchester railway opened
	Baltimore and Ohio railway opened
1832	Reform Act
	Cholera epidemic in Britain
	First French railway opened
1833	Factory Act dealing with employment of children in textile mills
	First all-steam crossing of the Atlantic by *Royal William*
1834	Grand National Consolidated Trades Union formed

1836	New patents law in United States
1839	Charles Goodyear invents the vulcanization of rubber
1842	Mines Act: women and girls banned from working underground
	Chadwick's *Report on the Sanitary Condition of the Labouring Population*
	Peel's government reforms the tariff
1846	Repeal of the Corn Laws
1846	Elias Howe patents a sewing machine in the United States
1847	Ten Hours Act
1851	The Great Exhibition at the Crystal Palace, London
1853	Gail Borden patents method of canning evaporated milk
1854–56	The Crimean War
1856	Parliament grants limited liability to companies engaged in production and trade
	Henry Bessemer develops process to improve the manufacture of steel
1860–65	Civil War in the United States
1867	Factory Acts Extension Act
	The Workshops Regulation Act

Some Suggestions for Further Reading

ASHTON, T. S.: *The Industrial Revolution*. Oxford, revised 1964.

CHITWOOD, Oliver P.: *A History of Colonial America*. New York: Harper, 1948.

COLE, G. D. H. & FILSON, A. W.: *British Working Class Movements: select documents 1789–1875*. Macmillan, 1965.

COURT, W. H. B.: *A Concise Economic History of Britain*. Cambridge, 1954.

DERRY, T. K. & WILLIAMS, T. I.: *A Short History of Technology*. Oxford, 1960.

EDWARDS, M. M.: *The Growth of the British Cotton Trade*. Manchester, 1967.

FAULKNER, H. U.: *American Economic History*. Harper & Brothers, 1954 (7th ed.).

GEORGE, Dorothy: *England in Transition*. Pelican, revised 1953.

GIBBS-SMITH, C. H.: *The Great Exhibition of 1851*. H.M.S.O., revised 1964.

GRAS, N. S. B.: *Industrial Evolution*. Cambridge: Harvard University Press, 1930.

HABAKKUK, H. J.: *American and British Technology in the Nineteenth Century*. Cambridge University Press, 1962.

HILLS, Richard L.: *Power in the Industrial Revolution*. Manchester, 1970.

HOBSBAWN, E. J.: *Industry and Empire*. Weidenfeld & Nicolson, 1968.

MANTOUX, P.: *The Industrial Revolution in the Eighteenth Century*. Jonathan Cape, revised 1961.

NORTH, Douglass C.: *The Economic Growth of the United States, 1790 to 1860*. Prentice-Hall, Inc., 1961.

OWEN, R.: *The Life of Robert Owen*, written by himself. London & Philadelphia, 1867.

PERKIN, H.: *The Origins of Modern English Society*. Routledge & Kegan Paul, 1969.

PIKE, E. Royston: *Human Documents of the Industrial Revolution in Britain*. George Allen & Unwin, 1966.

PINCHBECK, Ivy: *Women Workers and the Industrial Revolution*. Frank Cass, 1969.

REDFORD, A.: *The Economic History of Englano 1760–1860*. Longmans, 1931.

ROBERTSON, Ross M.: *History of the American Economy*. Harcourt, Brace & World, 1964 (2nd ed.).

ROOKE, P.: *The Growth of the Social Services*. Rupert Hart-Davis, 1968.

THOMAS, Malcolm I.: *The Luddites,* David and Charles (G.B.) Archon Books, Hamden, Connecticut (U.S.).

WARE, Caroline F.: *The Early New England Cotton Manufacture : a Study in Industrial Beginnings*. New York: Houghton Mifflin, 1931.

WARE, Norman J.: *The Industrial Worker, 1840–1860*. Boston: Houghton Mifflin, 1924.

WILLIAMSON, Harold F.: *The Growth of the American Economy*. Prentice-Hall, 1951.

WRIGHT, Chester W.: *Economic History of the United States*. New York: McGraw-Hill, 1949 (2nd ed.).

Index